Reconcilable Differences?

Reconcilable Differences?

Congress, the Budget Process,
and the Deficit

John B. Gilmour

UNIVERSITY OF CALIFORNIA PRESS
BERKELEY LOS ANGELES OXFORD

University of California Press
Berkeley and Los Angeles, California

University of California Press, Ltd.
Oxford, England

©1990 by
The Regents of the University of California

Library of Congress Cataloging-in-Publication Data
Gilmour, John B.
    Reconcilable differences?: Congress, the budget process,
and the deficit / John B. Gilmour.
        p. cm.
    Includes bibliographical references.
    ISBN 0-520-06778-9.   ISBN 0-520-06943-9 (pbk.)
    1. Budget—United States. 2. Budget deficits—United States.
    I. Title.
    HJ2051.G53 1990   89-27123
    353.0072′2—dc20   CIP

Printed in the United States of America
1   2   3   4   5   6   7   8   9

The paper used in this publication meets the minimum requirements of
American National Standard for Information Sciences—Permanence of
Paper for Printed Library Material, ANSI Z39.48-1984.⊗

For my mother and father

Contents

Preface

The federal budget deficit has raged out of control for almost a decade, despite the belief of both public officials and major economists that deficits are too large. When something goes so obviously wrong, invariably we seek to assign blame. Two familiar scapegoats are the budget process and "gutless" members of Congress. In this case there is probably enough blame to go around, but I believe it is unreasonable to accuse either inviting target.

This is a book about the congressional budget process, particularly the "reconciliation" process as part of the larger budget process. The perverse argument of this book is that the budget process is a success. It does not balance the budget, but no legislative procedure could accomplish that feat; instead, the process provides politicians with the tools they will need to implement a balanced budget—should the time come that they are able to agree on how to eliminate or substantially reduce the deficit. The great achievement of the process is to reduce much of the ability of factions within Congress to obstruct and delay legislation they find offensive. The weakness of the process is that only seldom are there majorities in Congress capable of substantially using the powerful tools now available to them.

Politicians engaged in public acts of self-flagellation often claim that the failure of Congress to balance the budget is due to a lack of the "guts," the "intestinal fortitude," or the "courage" needed to stand up to the "special interests" and vote for spending reductions. Such comments generally mean both that representatives are unwilling to vote against their immediate electoral interests and that they should be so willing. I find this an interesting contention. It is certainly true that if members of Congress were angels, it would be easier to reduce the deficit. But if we must depend on having virtuous individuals in office to enact decent public policy, then we are in deep, deep trouble. Moreover, the idea of relying on good elected officials for attaining good government is entirely at odds with our constitutional structure. Madison and other founding fathers, "realists" as they were, understood that selfish, venal individuals with very human failings would find their way into public office with some regularity; thus, they strove to erect a political structure that would operate satisfactorily even without angels to run it. I believe it behooves us still to strive for political structures that enable politicians to enact reasonable policies in the public interest without superhuman displays of courage. The congressional budget process is one such effort.

I have received assistance from many sources in writing this book. Nelson Polsby first suggested that I look at the reconciliation process, and as my study progressed he generously provided counsel. I am deeply grateful to him. Aaron Wildavsky was also very liberal with time and assistance. Joe White read the entire manuscript twice and improved it greatly. Nick Masters of the House Budget Committee helped me secure office space on Capitol Hill and also assisted by setting up some interviews. The willingness of participants in the budget process to take the time to explain to me what they did, and why, frequently amazed me; without their generosity this study could never have been written. The Institute of Governmental Studies of the University of California, Berkeley, provided funds that permitted my first interviews in Washington. The Brookings Institution provided a one-year graduate fellowship that greatly facilitated research and writing. Ann Kendrick, Jim Savage, Bob Katzmann, Kirk Brown, Cathy Johnson, Allen Schick, Raymond Wolfinger, Peter Schwartz, Eugene Bardach, Tom Hammond, Barry Ames, and Mark Kamlet all provided valuable help.

J. B. G.
St. Louis, Missouri
May 29, 1989

Introduction

In its dealings with budgetary issues since 1980, Congress has acted uncharacteristically, upsetting long-standing expectations and contradicting contemporary theories of congressional behavior. Members of Congress are seekers of reelection, we are told, and the quest to retain their offices leads them to decentralize the organization of Congress because, through their work in committees, representatives can best engage in the activities most likely to get them reelected. In policy making we have come to expect Congress and its members to favor legislation that confers tangible benefits upon constituents and districts, while scrupulously avoiding choices that impose costs or hardships directly upon constituents.

Despite these widespread expectations, members of Congress have undermined their committee system by developing an overarching, all-encompassing budget process that allows congressional majorities to exercise an unprecedented degree of control over committees. Moreover, since 1980 Congress has come to rely on budgetary negotiations and decision making that take place largely or entirely outside the normal committee structure of Congress. In some cases the budget process has

enabled congressional floor majorities to adopt comprehensive budgets on the floor and to enforce their preferences on reluctant committees. In other cases party
leadership and committee chairs have agreed on the
general outlines of budget policy and used the budget
process as a means of implementing these group decisions. Either way, the budget process disrupts the ordinary sequence of the legislative process. Normally the
committees go first, determining their own agenda and
presenting legislative proposals to the rest of the chamber. Under the new budget process entities outside committees—whether gatherings of committee chairs, summit meetings, or committed majorities—effectively can
set the agenda for committees and direct them to draft
spending resolutions or tax increases.

Two episodes from recent history suggest the nature
of the new budgetary order in Congress. First, in 1981,
the initial year of the Reagan presidency, a unanimous
Republican party in the House was joined by a substantial number of "boll weevil" Democrats; they succeeded
in enacting the president's budget recommendations in
their entirety, despite the objections of committees with
jurisdictions over programs and despite the best efforts
of the majority party leadership to thwart the administration's budget proposals. Republicans were able to
achieve this remarkable feat only because of the budget
process, particularly the new "reconciliation" procedure, which enormously consolidates congressional
procedure and reduces the influence of committees.

Second, spurred on by the Black Monday stock market crash of October 19, 1987, in which the Dow Jones
average fell by more than 500 points in one day, Democrats and Republicans of both the House and the Senate
met with leaders from the administration and negoti-

ated a package of deficit reductions worth some $30 billion. Committees in both chambers then proceeded to draft legislation implementing the decisions reached in the interbranch "summit" meetings. Such summit meetings, almost commonplace in the 1980s, were basically nonexistent before 1980. The initiation of reconciliation is linked with that of interbranch budgetary negotiations: reconciliation allows committed floor majorities to impose their will on committees, making it possible to enforce negotiated agreements. Without an enforcement device, it makes little sense to negotiate agreements.

These developments contrast starkly with Woodrow Wilson's classic discussion of Congress. A century ago, Wilson asserted that Congress conducts its "business by what may figuratively, but not inaccurately, be described as an odd device of *disintegration*." In Wilson's view, Congress qualified as "disintegrated" because its work was conducted by the parts—the committees— and not the whole. "Congress in session," he continued, "is Congress on public exhibition, whilst Congress in its committee-rooms is Congress at work." Furthermore, he wrote, "the chairmen of the Standing Committees do not constitute a cooperative body like a ministry. They do not consult and concur in the adoption of homogeneous and mutually helpful measures; there is no thought of acting in concert. Each committee goes its own way at its own pace."[1] Subsequent observers have seen little to cause them to disagree with Wilson's assessment. Innumerable observers of Congress have found it to be a committee-centered body in which negotiations are conducted in committee and important

1. Woodrow Wilson, *Congressional Government* (Gloucester, Mass.: Peter Smith, 1973), chap. 2, pp. 57–98.

decisions are not made on the floor. Authors often condemn the fragmented structure of Congress; sometimes they applaud it, and occasionally they are even ambivalent. But whatever view they take of fragmentation and committee autonomy, they do not dispute their existence.

There has also been common agreement on congressional policy-making tendencies. At least since Schattschneider wrote about the politics of the Smoot-Hawley tariff, scholars have contended that Congress favors narrow, assertive interests, over broader, less well-mobilized interests.[2] This tendency manifests itself in the congressional enthusiasm for water projects and public works,[3] agriculture subsidies, food stamps,[4] merchant marine subsidies, tariffs,[5] tax exclusions,[6] veterans' benefits, and Social Security.[7]

But in 1980, an election year, Congress did the unthinkable when it voted to increase taxes and cut spending. In 1981 Congress passed the largest spending cut ever enacted. In 1982 Congress defied conventional wis-

---

2. E. E. Schattschneider, *Politics, Pressure, and the Tariff* (New York: Prentice-Hall, 1935).

3. John A. Ferejohn, *Pork-Barrel Politics: Rivers and Harbors Legislation, 1947–1968* (Stanford: Stanford University Press, 1974).

4. John A. Ferejohn, "Logrolling in an Institutional Context: A Case Study of Food Stamp Legislation," in *Congress and Policy Change*, ed. Gerald Wright, Leroy Rieselbach, and Lawrence Dodd (New York: Agathon Press, 1986), pp. 223–253.

5. Schattschneider, *Politics, Pressure, and the Tariff*.

6. Stanley Surrey, "How Special Tax Provisions Get Enacted," *Harvard Law Review* 70 (1957): 1145–1182. Of course, the tax reform of 1986 suggests that tax politics is not necessarily controlled by those seeking tax expenditures. But the story of the 1986 tax bill fully confirms the view that members of Congress cater to special interests. Jeffrey Birnbaum and Allan Murray, *Showdown at Gucci Gulch* (New York: Random House, 1987).

7. Martha Derthick, *Policymaking for Social Security* (Washington, D.C.: Brookings Institution, 1979).

dom when it cut spending and enacted the largest tax increase in history. Normally we expect Congress to pass difficult legislation only with presidential support, but in passing the 1982 tax bill, the Tax Equity and Fiscal Responsibility Act, Congress and the president reversed roles, as the legislative branch persuaded an otherwise reluctant executive to go along with a large revenue increase. Again in 1983, 1984, 1985, and 1987, Congress passed legislation to cut spending and increase taxes.

Congress has achieved these perverse results by means of its budget process, enacted first in 1974 and variously strengthened in subsequent years. The overall effect has been to centralize congressional handling of the budget, increase the influence of congressional floor majorities, and reduce the autonomy of committees. The heart of the budget process has been the reconciliation procedure, first employed in 1980. Reconciliation, a revolutionary tool, enables congressional majorities to overcome barriers to swift and comprehensive action, dramatically reduces the long-standing capacity of committees to block the legislative desires of majorities, facilitates intercommittee negotiations, and, perhaps more important, increases the probability that the results of negotiations will be implemented. By means of reconciliation, congressional majorities can direct committees to reduce spending on the programs in their jurisdictions. It significantly reduces the virtual veto power committees have had over changes and reductions in entitlement programs, and this rearranges the balance of power between committee and chamber or between "faction" and "majority." Not in the past hundred years have majorities been so favored by congressional procedure and organization. Without the budget process, the budget cuts and tax increases enacted in

1980 and subsequent years almost certainly would not have been passed. Given what we have come to expect from Congress, this is truly, as James Jones (D-Okla.) claims, "the most bizarre way to legislate."[8]

New procedures do not, of course, appear of their own accord; rather they are adopted by Congress to enable its members to achieve purposes considered unattainable under previous arrangements. Procedure does not itself determine policy; rather it is the means by which members' preferences are translated into actual legislation, an intervening variable that influences and shapes the translation of members' policy preferences into legislation. Procedure can warp and modify the extent to which legislation reflects the preferences of representatives, but it cannot cause the enactment of legislation that members do not, in some sense, desire. Members can and do change the procedure of Congress when they perceive that it obstructs their will or otherwise produces undesirable consequences.

In this book, legislators are seen as complex individuals with conflicting preferences. They are concerned with both particular programs, especially those of disproportionate benefit to their own constituents, and such issues as the size of the budget, its distribution among programs, the size of the deficit and its impact on the economy, and the size of the total public debt, even though such issues may not be of direct electoral benefit and even when these goals interfere with the quest to obtain tangible benefits for their constituents. Legislators want more spending for their constituents, but they also want to balance the budget. Budgetary procedure mediates between the preferences of legisla-

8. *Congressional Record,* daily edition (June 25, 1981), p. H3390; hereafter cited *Cong. Rec.*

tors and their choices, helping to determine which preferences will be manifested in a given decision. A budgetary procedure that focuses more attention on the size of the budget and less on the components tends to elicit member preferences for lower spending. A procedure that focuses attention on particular programs tends to elicit member preferences for more spending. In budgetary matters, how a question is posed largely determines the answer given; consequently, budgetary procedure is of tremendous importance in "framing" issues.

Members of Congress recognize the impact of different procedural arrangements on their behavior. Consequently, when members discover that the budgets enacted by Congress diverge significantly from what they want, they will attempt to set matters straight—not by voting directly for a more suitable budget, but by changing the procedures under which they consider budgetary issues. This happened in 1974 and 1980: Congress found itself incapable of adopting acceptable budgets under its existing budget process, and so it amended its procedures in an effort to produce better budgets.

Since 1974 members of Congress have been seeking to create a set of budget procedures that will result in enacting a satisfactory budget. In this quest, they acted on the belief, widely shared among political scientists and other observers of Congress, that a major source of their problem was a budgetary organization and procedure that fragmented budgetary deliberations. By distributing power over spending to many committees and subcommittees, Congress gained considerable control over the parts of the budget but lost sight of the whole. According to this interpretation of congressional incapacity, the proper solution was to reconstitute congressional ability to control the budget as a whole.

Budget reforms have introduced procedure and organization that enable Congress to adopt a plan to balance or do anything else with the budget, should only members agree on such a plan. That cannot be said of any previous budgetary arrangements in Congress, which could and did prevent enacting coherent budget policy in Congress. The ability to adopt and implement a budget plan in Congress may seem to some a minimal or trivial accomplishment, but it is without precedent in the annals of the modern Congress. In this sense—political or structural—I would argue that the budget process has been a success. This book documents and explains political and structural changes that have taken place in Congress in the 1980s as a result of the budget process.

The magnitude of change has been difficult to appreciate because of the concurrent rise of extremely large budget deficits, which have arisen and persisted despite the apparent opposition of nearly every member of Congress and the president. A casual examination of the history of budget deficits and budget reform might lead one to believe that budget reform encourages not increased congressional control of the budget, but instead large deficits. In the twenty years before the adoption of the Budget Act in 1974, deficits were common but normally small, and debt declined continuously as a percentage of GNP throughout this period (see Figures 1 and 2). But soon after implementing the budget process the deficit began regularly to exceed $50 billion, and debt ceased to decline as a percentage of GNP. Then, after the process was significantly strengthened in 1980 through introducing the reconciliation procedure, the deficit promptly surpassed first $100 billion and then $200 billion. If correlation could be interpreted as causation, the budget process would be considered one of the great ca-

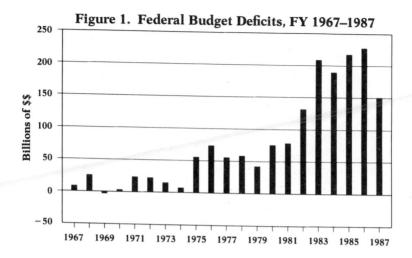

Figure 1. Federal Budget Deficits, FY 1967–1987

Figure 2. Total Federal Debt as a Percentage of GNP, FY 1963–1985

tastrophes of all time because efforts to make it stronger have consistently been accompanied by increases in the deficit.

Observers often dismiss the budget process as ineffective and interpret the fantastic increase in the deficit during the life of the budget process as evidence of failure. President Reagan called the process "a sorry spectacle . . . a magic show. It's wink and blink; and smoke and mirrors; and pulling rabbits out of hats; but almost all that ever comes up are designs to hide increases for special interests."[9] Detractors point out that Congress, faced with $200 billion deficits "as far as the eye can see,"[10] passes spending cuts of only $10 billion or even less. Furthermore, to produce this morsel of savings the budget process drags on for months past supposed deadlines, disrupts normal legislative activity, compels reliance on continuing resolutions rather than normal appropriations bills, and generally turns Congress inside out.

Assessing the impact of a procedural change solely or primarily by means of budgetary outputs grossly oversimplifies the relationship between procedure and outcomes. The massive deficits of the Reagan era and the frustrating inability of Congress and the president to eliminate them do not indicate procedural inadequacies in Congress as much as a failure of the House, the Senate, and the president to agree on a specific means of reducing the deficit. Both the House and the Senate have proposed major deficit reduction plans that have stalled because of either an inability of the two chambers to agree or threatened presidential vetoes. Likewise, the president has proposed significant cuts in domestic programs, but he has been unable to convince Congress to enact them. The problem is that neither the White

9. *Reform of the Federal Budget Process*, Hearings before the House Committee on Government Operations, 100th Cong., 1st sess. (USGPO, 1987), p. 195.

10. David Stockman is responsible for this unsettling description of the budget dilemma. *The Triumph of Politics* (New York: Harper & Row, 1986), p. 370.

House, the budget committees, nor anyone else has been able to devise a plan to reduce the deficit that will satisfy both chambers of Congress and the president. If and when that plan appears, the budgetary procedure of Congress will facilitate its enactment into law. We have witnessed less a failure of the budget process than a lesson in separation of powers. Overcoming problems like these demands reducing conflict in government, not tinkering with procedures.[11]

Similarly, observers take the passage of Gramm-Rudman, the automatic budget balancing bill, as evidence of the failure of the budget process. Frustrated with the persistence of huge deficits, Congress twice adopted measures that set mandatory deficit reduction targets and required automatic reductions in spending if Congress was unable to meet deficit targets. In fact, Gramm-Rudman neither subverts nor replaces the budget process; indeed, it complements the process well. The threat of large, across-the-board reductions in all programs, except a handful specifically exempted, was intended to create a strong incentive on the part of Congress and the president to agree on a deficit reduction package. When and if such deficit reduction packages are negotiated, the reconciliation procedure is nearly the only practical, workable means of implementing them.

The budget process should enable Congress to exert control over the level and growth of spending where there is a clear preference to do so. This it has done. Even though the budget deficit has often been huge since

11. See James L. Sundquist, *Constitutional Reform and Effective Government* (Washington, D.C.: Brookings Institution, 1986), who argues for lessening separation of powers on the grounds that it will reduce stalemate.

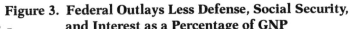

Figure 3. Federal Outlays Less Defense, Social Security, and Interest as a Percentage of GNP

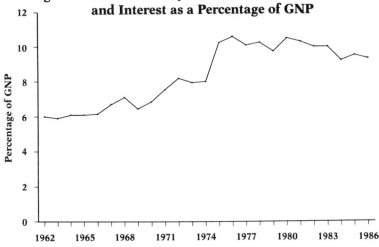

1974, it nonetheless appears that congressional behavior in some respects has been very responsible. An examination of expenditure growth from the 1960s through the 1980s suggests that Congress has exerted rather tight control over large portions of the budget following the adoption of the Budget Act. Since 1974 spending has continued to grow in relation to Gross National Product. But if we exclude three especially high priority components of the budget—defense, Social Security, and interest on the national debt, all of which have deliberately been protected from budgetary control—we can see evidence of congressional restraint. Figure 3 shows federal outlays, minus defense, Social Security, and interest, as a percentage of GNP. For twenty years prior to FY 1976 the remaining components of the budget rose rapidly and continuously in relation to GNP.

However, after instituting the budget process there has been no growth and even a small decline. An examination of spending in the same budget functions ex-

**Figure 4. Outlays Less Defense, Social Security, and
Interest, in Constant 1967 Dollars**

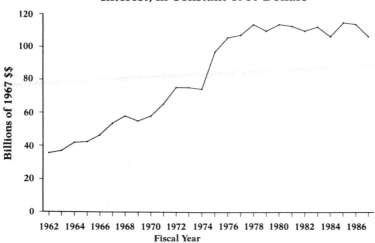

pressed in constant 1967 dollars shows a steady increase
prior to FY 1976, but only a very gradual increase thereafter (see Figure 4). The exempted budget functions are
very large, but those remaining include all other payments to individuals, Medicare and Medicaid, public
works, civil service compensation and retirement, veterans' benefits, and so on. In these areas of the budget,
at least, a strong tendency toward growth has been
countered, and spending has not been out of control. In
the case of Social Security and defense, there has been a
strong consensus that growth should occur. A budget
process cannot, and should not, obstruct the will of Congress. But where Congress has willed restraint, it has
been able to achieve it through the process. These data
pose a significant challenge to critics who blithely dismiss the budget process as ineffectual.

Chapter 1 of this book studies the background of the
Budget Act. In the years prior to adopting the Budget

Act, Congress was continually of two minds over the budget, voting for both more spending on particular programs and a lower overall total. The chaotic situation thus engendered led to the adoption of the new process.

Chapter 2 discusses the budget process and how it addresses the problems discussed in the first chapter. I argue that by creating a more consolidated budget process, involving the simultaneous consideration of both the parts and the whole, the new process tends to discourage the flip-flop characteristic of the preceding years.

Chapter 3 shows how the actual use of the budget process and how the introduction of reconciliation in 1980 have caused a major transfer of power out of committees. I argue that power in the budget process is not exercised by the normal legislative committees, or even by the budget committees, but rather by the majority coalitions that form to pass budget resolutions. Insofar as majorities are able to agree on policy, the budget process with reconciliation allows them to get their way. This is a degree of majoritarianism unknown in Congress since the days of Joe Cannon.

Chapter 4 examines the impact of the budget process on congressional committees. Formerly committees would "go their own way at their own speed." Under the budget process, however, congressional committees find their actions constrained by an array of scheduling and reporting requirements, as well as by spending ceilings and required reconciliation legislation in conformity with a budget resolution. Committees lose much of their autonomy and become part of a more tightly integrated Congress.

Chapter 5 discusses the Gramm-Rudman phenomenon. In 1985 Congress enacted a law requiring the budget to be balanced by fiscal year 1991 and authorizing the president to withhold, or "sequester," sufficient funds to achieve that goal. Congress resorted to such a radical solution to the problem of persistent deficits due to the unwillingness of the president and Congress to come to terms on a plan to produce lower deficits. Through the experience of Gramm-Rudman we can see more clearly why the budget process, despite its marvelous majoritarian features, has not produced more nearly balanced budgets. President Reagan insisted on maintaining low tax rates and high defense spending, while Democrats in Congress wanted to cut defense, increase taxes, and protect domestic programs. They could not agree on a course of action, and so the budget process could be of little use. Gramm-Rudman was a plan to force consensus by threatening massive and destructive program cuts in the absence of action to reduce the deficit. By the end of the Reagan administration it had done little to force consensus.

1

Confusion in Budgetary Politics, 1966–1972

From 1966 to 1972 Congress found itself caught in a budgetary swamp from which there was no easy escape. Torn between its members' desires to increase funding for popular programs and their wish to avoid spending growth and deficits, Congress voted alternately for both increases in programs and overall decreases in spending. Representatives want many things from the budget, yet a cruel mathematics governs budgeting and prevents Congress from increasing programs without allowing overall spending growth. Rationality would seem to dictate that, given conflicting preferences, individuals should consult their consciences, their stars, their relatives—or in the case of legislators, their constituents—and seek to resolve conflicts in some coherent way. Rational behavior consists not in choosing any particular set of issues but in balancing competing preferences.[1] Congressional behavior was irrational in these

1. Russell Hardin discusses this conception of rationality: "One is rational if, after considering all of one's concerns—moral, altruistic,

years because members did not resolve conflicts and voted in contradictory and inconsistent ways, producing an irresponsible overall policy. This behavior likewise produced an institutional crisis of major proportions.

The crisis of 1966 to 1972 followed a period of relative calm. For many years the budgetary system, described by Richard Fenno and Aaron Wildavsky, centered upon a strong House Appropriations Committee; it admirably restrained member demands for increasing expenditures on particular programs and maintained near budgetary balance.[2] For the two decades after World War II, Congress had, and its members supported, institutions that enabled Congress to produce budgets that were largely acceptable in both their distribution of spending to programs and the total. This was a remarkable achievement, especially given the turmoil that was soon to follow. By the mid-1960s that system of "preference regulation" was beginning to decline, and as it went Congress lost its capacity to balance demands; a period of extremely high conflict marked by erratic and inconsistent congressional behavior resulted.

Frustration in Congress led nearly every year to the

---

familial, narrowly self-interested, and so forth—one then chooses coherently in trading each off against the others. . . . Another way of conceiving this notion is to suppose that one's mind is compartmentalized, that one is a synthesis of several selves, each concerned with particular material and all governed by an overall regulator who, in making present choices of how to act, assigns systematic weights to all the selves, according as they have already been more or less differentially satisfied. One could meaningfully say of such a regulator that it was rational or irrational." Hardin, *Collective Action* (Baltimore: Johns Hopkins University Press for Resources for the Future, 1982), p. 10.

2. Richard Fenno, *The Power of the Purse* (Boston: Little, Brown, 1966); Aaron Wildavsky, *The Politics of the Budgetary Process* (Boston: Little, Brown, 1964).

enactment of a binding spending ceiling that gave the executive branch power to cut spending. Congress could agree on a spending total but not on distributing those expenditures among programs as it had done before; thus, Congress was compelled to transfer to the executive branch a vast chunk of its greatest legislative power, the "power of the purse."

The problem in Congress was not simply that its members voted spending increases, but that after voting for increases they became dissatisfied with the overall size of the budget and then voted to reduce the total— without cutting individual programs. The budget battles of 1966–1972 were so wrenching precisely because Congress was constantly of two minds over the budget: supporting the programs and opposing the total. Its conflicted state of mind led Congress to contradict itself repeatedly. By voting alternately for more spending and then for less spending Congress undermined its institutional authority and showed itself incapable of producing coherent policy on its own. Had Congress stood unequivocally behind the programs it funded and accepted the total to which they added, there would have been no crisis in Congress. The legislative and executive branches would have differed over policy, with President Nixon demanding lower spending and Congress disagreeing, but that is perfectly ordinary in a system of separated powers and should not be interpreted as an institutional crisis. The remarkable feature of this period was not that the president criticized Congress but that many senators and representatives agreed with the president when he denounced Congress.[3]

3. According to Louis Fisher, in *Presidential Spending Power* (Princeton, N.J.: Princeton University Press, 1975), "most members of Congress even outdid the President in decrying the irresponsibility of Congress" (p. 175).

Structural and Procedural Fragmentation

In 1972 President Nixon denounced what he called "hoary and traditional procedure of the Congress, which now permits action on the various spending programs as if they were unrelated and independent actions."[4] Much of the difficulty Congress experienced in producing a budget was attributed to its fragmented budgetary system, which was organized in such a way as to virtually preclude considering a budgetary total and to prevent considering individual spending items in the context of an overall budget policy. Spending authority was fragmented among many committees, and revenue decisions likewise were considered wholly separate from expenditure decisions.

Separate Consideration of Taxing and Spending

Until the 1860s the House Ways and Means Committee maintained jurisdiction over both revenue and expenditure legislation. After the Civil War, authority over spending was given to the newly formed Appropriations Committee, and ever since these responsibilities have always been divided.[5] With the exception of a minor, short-lived experiment after World War II, there has been a complete absence of formal coordination between these two committees. Tax legislation would and still does originate in the House Committee on Ways and Means and the Senate Committee on Finance. Spending

4. Quoted in Fisher, *Presidential Spending Power,* p. 175.

5. See Joint Study Committee on Budget Control, *Recommendations for Improving Congressional Control Over Budgetary Outlay and Receipt Totals,* 93rd Cong., 1st sess., H. Rept. 93–147 (USGPO, 1973), p. 9. Two years after the House divided these taxing and spending responsibilities in 1867, the Senate did likewise.

and taxing are, of course, related, yet congressional organization did not recognize this simple fiscal fact. In the event of a deficit, the tax committees could argue that spending committees had spent too much, while the spending committees could contend that the tax committees had cut taxes too much. There was no institutional recognition of the deficit, which fell into the jurisdiction of no committee. Each year decisions would be made about spending and taxing, but never were these decisions formally integrated or coordinated. Consequently the deficit was merely the difference between revenue and expenditure, never the object of an explicit decision. Thus, members of Congress would explain, the deficit simply "happened."

A legislator who became concerned with the deficit and wished to exert some control over that policy outcome had no ready or direct means of doing so, largely because the deficit was the product of hundreds of other decisions each year and Congress lacked the power to control the size of the deficit directly. This feature distinguishes the deficit from nearly any other issue. Normally an individual who sought influence over a particular policy area—veterans' affairs or agriculture, for instance—could do so quite easily, by obtaining a seat on either the Veterans or Agriculture committees. In these cases the structure of Congress aids members who wish to specialize by policy area. The budget deficit is no less important a policy issue than veterans' affairs or agriculture, but no single committee or other entity within Congress was responsible for it. To influence the deficit, a member of Congress would have to prevail in dozens and dozens of decisions each year in every policy area, while someone concerned with other, more discrete policy areas had a much simpler task. Budgetary structure and organization was almost certain to frustrate and overwhelm the member with a particular concern for the deficit.

Entitlement Spending

Government programs and federal agencies have traditionally been financed by means of annual appropriations. Congress enacts appropriations each year in thirteen regular appropriations bills plus assorted supplemental appropriations. These grants of spending authority are for the most part very specific as to the amount of money and purposes for which it can be used. Appropriations are beneficial from the standpoint of expenditure control, for they embody a mild bias against spending: unless a program receives its annual appropriation from both the House and the Senate, it ceases to exist; unless Congress votes affirmatively to increase the funding level of a program, it cannot grow.

Entitlements are the other principal means of funding programs, and they tend to subvert budgetary control. Entitlement programs generally provide cash benefits directly to individuals who meet certain criteria specified in legislation.[6] Anyone falling into the designated categories (disabled, old, unemployed, etc.) is "entitled" by law to receive benefits at a level also established by law. The actual outlays for an entitlement program are thus determined by factors outside immediate congres-

6. An excellent treatment of entitlements is R. Kent Weaver, "Controlling Entitlements," in *The New Direction in American Politics*, John Chubb and Paul Peterson (Washington, D.C.: Brookings Institution, 1985). "Entitlement," "appropriations," and other technical budgeting terms are explained in *A Glossary of Terms Used in the Federal Budget Process*, 3d ed. (Washington, D.C.: General Accounting Office, 1981).

sional control. If the economy goes into recession, more people will qualify for unemployment and welfare benefits, and the costs of these programs will rise accordingly. Consequently, expenditures on these programs can and do rise and fall without any direct congressional action or approval.[7] The existence of entitlements does not depend on passing an annual appropriation or reauthorization, and thus spending continues unabated until legislation making some alteration passes.

Unlike appropriations, entitlements benefit from a bias in favor of their continuation because legislation must be passed to curtail or otherwise change them. Entitlements also grant the committee with jurisdiction over them much power because they can, by refusing to consider or report legislation to change their programs, practically ensure the continuation of the status quo. The same logic applies to tax expenditures. Tax expenditures, or tax loopholes, are provisions of law that reduce tax liability for individuals who satisfy criteria specified in legislation. Like entitlements, tax expenditures remain as is and continue to reduce tax revenues until new legislation is passed changing them.[8] Both entitlements and tax expenditures increase the power of minorities within Congress (in the form of committees) and reduce the capacity of congressional majorities to prevail. The discharge petition was adopted for the pur-

7. Many of the largest entitlements are indexed to inflation, which means that benefits rise with the cost of living. However, cost of living allowances were often calculated in such a manner that benefits frequently rose faster than inflation, and this greatly exacerbated problems of budgetary control. In the 1980s, cost of living allowances have been recalculated to restrain the rate of automatic growth.

8. See Stanley Surrey and Paul McDaniel, *Tax Expenditures* (Cambridge: Harvard University Press, 1985), for the definitive treatment of this topic.

pose of enabling majorities to overcome committee intransigence, but it has never proven highly effective as a means of subjecting committees to majority control.

The Closed Character of the Taxing and Spending Committees

The Ways and Means and Appropriations committees in the House have long enjoyed various procedural and other advantages that have enabled these committees to maintain an unusual degree of independence and have also limited the extent to which the rest of the House could control budget policy.

The fragmentation of appropriations into multiple bills constitutes a significant problem. Most annual appropriations are contained in thirteen bills, one emerging from each of the thirteen subcommittees of the Appropriations Committee. The structure of the House and Senate committees are identical in this regard. By tradition these bills originated in the House, where they were reported by the Appropriations Committee one by one in serial fashion. Often, one bill was passed by the House before the next was out of committee. This practice helped maintain peace within the committee by focusing attention on the details of spending policy and distracting attention from the broad outline of fiscal policy.[9] The practice of serial consideration of appropriations also prevented members of Congress from comprehending the total size of the budget upon which they were voting. They did not vote upon the total, only on the individual bills, a practice that discouraged eval-

9. Richard F. Fenno, Jr., "The House Appropriations Committee as a Political System: The Problem of Integration," *American Political Science Review* 56 (June 1962): 310–324.

uating the worth of individual programs in the context of total spending. Not having two or more bills up for simultaneous consideration discouraged a "guns versus butter" comparison of relative budget priorities.

Splitting the budget into numerous segments prevented the emergence of a partisan or ideological battle over the budget. Appropriations bills ordinarily passed Congress with the support of huge majorities of both parties, without any amendments. The absence of partisanship in pork-barrel politics might be understandable. But is there any other democracy where the budget has not been a partisan issue? Normally we might expect the budget to be the single most partisan political issue, as it is in Britain where governments can fall over the budget. Fragmenting the budget in Congress distracts attention from grand questions of ideology and suppresses partisan conflict. It also makes the budget easier to pass. Fragmentation organizes conflict out of the budget, leaving Congress ill-equipped to exercise deliberate control over such crucial political issues as the size of the budget and the distribution of government spending among competing priorities.

In this period Congress as a whole could exert influence on the Appropriations Committee primarily by amending appropriations bills on the floor. This has not afforded an effective tool for manipulating appropriations policy, largely because members of Congress who are not on the Appropriations Committee have been poorly equipped to question the decisions of the committee. Under the rules of the House, appropriations bills are "privileged," which means they are always in order for floor consideration. For many years appropriations bills went directly to the floor from the Appropriations Committee, without passing through the Rules

Committee and often coming up for debate and vote before the printed committee report was available.[10] The unavailability of the committee report and the swiftness with which the vote was typically held restricted the information available to legislators not on the Appropriations Committee and impaired their ability to question the committee's actions. The Appropriations Committee, meanwhile, was an extremely bipartisan committee that engaged mostly in consensual decision making. Committee norms encouraged members to keep their grievances within the committee and not to offer amendments on the floor. Typically when an appropriations bill would come to the floor the subcommittee chair and the ranking minority member would engage in a "love feast," complimenting each other on their magnificent performance in producing the bill.[11] If members of the Appropriations Committee do little on the floor but praise each other and the bill, offer no amendments, and file no minority reports, other members of the House are deprived of valuable sources of information. Subsequent rules changes required committee reports to be published in advance of floor consideration, lessening the informational problems of would-be critics; still, the Appropriations Committee has occupied a rather dominating position in debate, given its command of the details of budgets and its ability to reach internal agreement.

The amendment of appropriations bills is relatively ineffective as a means of influencing overall budget pol-

10. Arthur MacMahon, "Congressional Oversight of Administration," *Political Science Quarterly* 58 (June 1943):161–190; 58 (September 1943): 380–414.
11. Fenno, *Power of the Purse.*

icy or spending levels. To achieve a reduction of, say, $10 billion, one would have to reduce dozens or even hundreds of line items. That is not an inviting task. Rather than endlessly debate the innumerable details of spending policy on the floor, proponents of spending reductions have instead sought to pass across-the-board percentage cuts in appropriations bills—for example, cutting every item in the Labor-HEW appropriation by 10 percent. This approach has the advantage of consuming little time and requiring no particular expertise, but it is a "meat ax" approach to spending reduction, cutting the good with the bad, even though no one would pretend that all categories of spending equally deserve to be cut. The bluntness of the across-the-board approach contrasts sharply with the high value the House Appropriations Committee normally attaches to expertise in policy making.

The complexity of congressional budgeting shattered any notion of responsibility or collective accountability. Congress as a whole never decided or voted upon the size of the budget, the volume of revenues, or the magnitude of the deficit; numerous committees within Congress had control over spending policy; and there was no formal coordination between revenue and expenditure. Budget policy was simply the amalgamation of a multitude of uncoordinated decisions, and overall budget policy was never the product of an explicit choice.

Viewed from the perspective of the whole political system, such fragmentation seems clearly destructive, but it nonetheless serves the purposes of individual members of Congress. Budgetary decentralization enables legislators to seek benefits for their constituents and to claim credit for those activities. It also allows them to avoid being held responsible for the collective consequences of their behavior—increased expenditures and rising deficits.

Regulation of Preferences by the Appropriations Committee

By 1972, Congress's budget system was performing poorly, but at one time it had performed admirably. Somehow, the fragmented institutions just described enabled Congress to produce acceptable budgets for many years. To understand why members of Congress later sought to eliminate or reduce fragmentation in budgeting and create a more centralized system, we must first explain how a fragmented system had managed to perform so effectively in the years between World War II and the mid-1960s.

Despite a complete absence of formal coordination within Congress, revenue and expenditure decisions were nonetheless relatively well-coordinated, and deficits were normally quite small. In the twenty years after World War II, only three times was the deficit larger than $10 billion, and most of the time it was less than $5 billion. A decentralized system was not perfect for all purposes, but it was adequate for most. Bickering would occasionally break out between the Ways and Means Committee and the Appropriations Committee over which committee was most responsible for the deficit. Overall, however, the level of conflict generated by this system was low.

The careful use of various "institutional maintenance" devices kept the lack of central control from producing a fiscal disaster.[12] Budgetary authority was neither unified in a single committee nor widely dispersed. Nearly all spending authority was under the jurisdiction of one committee in each chamber, and all revenue authority was controlled by one committee per chamber. These committees, moreover, were governed by an ethos that encouraged responsible behavior.[13]

The division of responsibility between authorizing and appropriating committees also tended to prevent irresponsible behavior. For most programs and agencies, there is a dual committee structure. Authorizing committees—such as Interior, Agriculture, Veterans, Energy and Commerce, Post Office, and Civil Service—pass legislation establishing agencies and programs, stipulating the purposes they ought to strive for, and authorizing agencies to spend money for those specified purposes. But their legislation, called "authorizations," does not itself provide any money. Only appropriations do that.[14] Advocates of agriculture or veterans' causes tend to gravitate to the authorizing committees where they can work most directly on matters of greatest interest to them and where they can recommend tremendous increases for the programs they favor most. But they have only the power to recommend increases, while the power to appropriate the funds remains with the Appropriations Committee. Members of the Appropriations

12. David Mayhew, *Congress: The Electoral Connection* (New Haven: Yale University Press, 1974).

13. See MacMahon, "Congressional Oversight of Administration"; and Fenno, "House Appropriations Committee."

14. For a detailed explanation of the relationship between authorizations and appropriations, see Louis Fisher, "The Authorizations-Appropriation Process in Congress: Formal Rules and Informal Practices," *Catholic Law Review* 29 (1979): 52–105.

Committee traditionally came from relatively safe districts; they, rather than their more vulnerable colleagues, could usually ignore the pleadings of constituents and thus act to hold down appropriations. The Appropriations Committee in the House was further insulated from pressures to spend by the "Cannon-Taber" rule, according to which members of the committee were appointed to subcommittees where they would not be dealing directly with the interests of their own constituents, allowing them to exercise more impartiality when considering requests.[15] The Appropriations Committee thus acted as a "saucer to cool the legislative tea," restraining the enthusiasm of the authorizing committees. Overall, authorizations have vastly exceeded actual appropriations, and members of authorizing committees have frequently been deeply annoyed when the Appropriations Committee gave their programs only a fraction of the recommended amount—or, in some cases, appropriated nothing at all to programs. Balancing program advocates against budgetary guardians helped provide a reasonable balancing of concerns for the total against concerns for the parts.

The Appropriations Committee could exercise their guardianship function and thwart the desires of other committees only because other members of the House wanted them to. There was nothing immutable about

15. See Fenno, *Power of the Purse*, pp. 138–143. Fenno reports two opposing tendencies. He reports that assignments were made on the basis of constituency interest but also asserts the existence of a countervailing tendency to appoint where there was no constituency interest. There seem to have been differences by subcommittee. The Agriculture subcommittee normally had a chair from an agricultural district, while the Public Works chair was usually from east of the Mississippi River.

the power of the House Appropriations Committee, and at any time a majority in the House could have voted to strip it of its powers or to overturn its decisions on the floor. The failure of the authorizing committees to rise up and destroy the Appropriations Committee, or simply to amend its bills regularly, indicates that the members were not concerned solely with maximizing expenditures for their constituents. Individual legislators frequently disagreed with particular decisions made by the Appropriations Committee, but their disappointment must have been overshadowed by a recognition that the committee performed a valuable service for Congress by controlling spending. Members of Congress would have liked to offer and pass amendments to appropriations bills, but they must have believed that for all members to get exactly what they wanted would have produced a disaster. Although an individual member would not get all he wanted for the program most valued by his constituents, neither did anyone else. Moreover, most programs would receive incremental increases that were large enough to keep Congress from rebelling against the tyranny of the Appropriations Committee. Through this system Congress was able to make a budget that was largely acceptable in both its total and deficit, as well as in its distribution of funding among programs. That was a significant achievement, enabling Congress to be a strong and independent force in policy making.

For various reasons, some internal to Congress and others external, the capacity of the congressional budgeting system to manage this balance between the total and the parts had decreased. By the mid- to late 1960s, the ability of the appropriations and tax committees to control budget policy declined, spending and the deficit grew, and conflict within Congress rose, signaling the onset of what Allen Schick quite aptly calls the "seven year budget war."[16]

Chief among the external causes of budgetary disruption was a slowing of economic growth that reduced revenue growth. A healthy economy minimizes budgetary conflict because everyone can have it all, or nearly so: the budget can be balanced, existing programs can grow, and new programs can be added, all without requiring increased taxes. When revenue growth declined it was no longer possible to satisfy all preferences on the budget, and latent conflict manifested itself with increasing frequency. The Vietnam War was also a major disruption of budgetary peace. In 1965, shortly after the enactment of major Great Society programs, President Johnson introduced U.S. combat forces in Vietnam, dramatically increasing the cost of the war. The combination of major domestic and foreign policy initiatives put enormous pressure on the budget.

The principal internal cause of disruption was an increasing fragmentation of budgetary authority in Congress. Ironically, just when the potential for budgetary conflict was rising rapidly—and when the need for controls on the total was growing—Congress reduced its capacity to handle that conflict. The decentralization of spending power in the 1960s occurred because the growth of entitlements effectively reduced the jurisdiction of the Appropriations Committee and gave direct spending power to the authorizing committees. In the case of most entitlement programs the Appropriations Committee has no practical control, leaving decisions

16. Allen Schick, *Congress and Money* (Washington, D.C.: Urban Institute, 1980), chap. 2.

about spending levels in the hands of programs advocates and reducing downward pressure on spending.

Over time the purposes pursued by the federal government have shifted progressively from the purchase of goods and services to payments to individuals; and as the functions of the government changed, so did the method of financing programs. Whether inadvertent or intentional, the growth of entitlement spending undeniably diminished the jurisdiction of the Appropriations Committee. In FY 1964 purchases of goods and services constituted 56.2 percent of all outlays; by FY 1975 that had declined to 36.1 percent. Over the same period transfer payments grew from 25.3 percent to 40.7 percent of outlays.[17] The diminution of the Appropriations Committee's jurisdiction left Congress without any committee or entity that could reasonably be held responsible for the budgetary total. This was a development of enormous significance. When the Appropriations Committee had jurisdiction over the vast bulk of federal spending, budgetary power was relatively concentrated. Following years in which there had been too large a deficit, the Appropriations Committee could exert a general downward influence on spending. Throughout the 1960s the congressional system for controlling the budget became increasingly outmoded and inadequate to control entitlements, the fastest growing portion of the budget.

Decentralized control of spending led to a crisis in the mid-1960s. Each of many committees wrote and reported legislation creating new programs or increasing spending on existing ones. Because no committee had responsibility for the total, none felt any responsibility

17. Ibid., p. 28.

to restrain their committee recommendations in the interests of reducing the overall total. Under these circumstances deficit control became something of a free rider problem: it was in everyone's interest to keep the deficit from becoming too large, but in no particular committee's interest or power to do anything about it. With more committees contributing to spending growth, some collective action would be required to curb it, but Congress had no means for producing collective action among its committees.

The entire chamber, acting on the floor to consider and amend bills, was not an adequate substitute for a diligent Appropriations Committee with nearly comprehensive jurisdiction over spending. Given a weakened Appropriations Committee and more widely spread spending authority, members of Congress found themselves facing a continuing stream of spending bills, each of which would have some unascertained impact on the total. Individual members' previously limited ability to influence the total was now almost completely vitiated; they could quite easily influence a particular program, by getting themselves assigned to the committee with jurisdiction over it. But there was no committee with jurisdiction over the total; the only way a member could express concern for the size of the budget was by voting against particular programs—a prospect most members of Congress found uninviting. This budgetary structure still regulated preferences, but it impeded expression of concern for the whole and afforded a strong position to those who favored spending increases. By the mid-1960s, House Republicans were becoming disturbed by the persistence of deficits and the rapid rate of budgetary growth, and they sought to reduce spending. However, because budgetary structure discouraged the enactment of spending reductions, they were forced to employ unusual means.

Efforts to Cut Appropriations

In 1965, the last year covered by Fenno's study of the appropriations process, we can see the beginnings of heightened budgetary conflict. All sixteen Republicans on the House Appropriations Committee signed a minority view to the committee report on a Labor-HEW supplemental bill. Such a revolt against the committee norms of unanimity on the floor was unusual. In floor debate, Melvin Laird (R-Wis.) of the Appropriations Committee moved to recommit the bill to committee, saying: "In substantial degree, we are entering once again a period when a choice must be made between guns and butter."[18] In 1965, at least, no choice was made, as the motion was soundly defeated by a vote of 139–263; all northern Democrats voted against recommittal.

The next year House Republicans undertook more systematically to hold down spending. Dissatisfied with both the total amount of federal outlays and the rate of growth, Frank Bow (R-Ohio), the ranking minority member on the Appropriations Committee, along with other Republicans on the Appropriations Committee, offered motions to recommit six appropriations bills, all with instructions to the committee to add language directing the president to spend no more than 95 percent of the total amount in the bill. Had these measures passed, Congress would have required the president to

18. *Congressional Quarterly Almanac, 1965* (Washington, D.C.: CQ Press, 1966), p. 167; hereafter cited *CQ Almanac.*

cut 5 percent from each bill so amended. No recommittal motion passed in 1966, although some received a significant measure of support, particularly from Republicans. House Republicans employed the same strategy the following year with seven appropriations bills. Two recommittal motions passed in 1967, requiring reductions of 5 percent in both the Transportation and the State, Justice, Commerce appropriations bills.

Defending the recommittal motions on the floor, Bow carefully explained that he was attacking no particular program, only the total. He offered no suggestions about how the 5 percent ought to be cut; yet he expressed confidence that the executive branch should easily be able to do the job. He proposed quite candidly that Congress pass the buck to the executive: "So we are not taking out projects but are simply saying to the Department of the Interior . . . you find the money." Bow was adamant about not descending to the level of the specific. "We are not attacking a single item in the bill. It is simply a reduction of the total amount."[19]

Critics of this novel approach to expenditure reduction would constantly ask where and how the cuts would be made. How could they vote for reductions without knowing the programmatic consequences? Silvio Conte (R-Mass.), also a member of the Appropriations Committee, opposed unspecified percentage reductions and pressed Bow to explain how the reductions should be made. Cavalierly, Bow brushed aside this criticism: "I would say to my colleague, he is using that cliché—where are you going to cut [?]"[20] The critics of the appropriations bills stressed the size of the bills and

19. *Cong. Rec.*, April 5, 1966, p. 7658.
20. Ibid., April 6, 1966, p. 7779.

the rate of growth. They neither found fault with the specifics of the spending nor denounced it as wasteful. Their only criticism was that the budget was becoming too big. The supporters of the recommittal motions carefully avoided being lured into debates about the causes of the increases, and they did not criticize the work of the Appropriations Committee.[21]

In 1967, when Charles Raper Jonas (R-N.C.) sought to reduce the size of the Treasury–Post Office bill, he began his assault with lavish praise for the members of that subcommittee. "Mr. Chairman, I was impressed by the thoroughness with which members of the committee had examined the budget requests and the discrimination they displayed in the markup of the bill." Jonas felt the committee had done a good job of examining and cutting administration budget requests, and he confessed that he did not know how to improve on the committee's work. "I do not know how additional cuts can be made," he explained.[22] He criticized only the growth of the bill by $797 million over the previous year. Jonas did not inquire into the causes of that rapid growth, but supporters of the bill pointed out the reasons, which they claimed were well justified. Most growth, they explained, was due to a large increase in postal pay that

21. Republicans seem much more inclined than Democrats to propose cuts without knowing what they will do. In 1947 House Republicans, then the majority, sought to cut spending by $6 billion. George Mahon, then as later, criticized the proposal on the grounds that no facts supported it. John Taber, the chairman of the Appropriations Committee in the House, said "we have not drawn these numbers out of a hat, but have a good idea of what we are basing them upon." Senate Republicans disagreed and admitted they had no basis for proposing a $6 billion cut rather than any other size. See Joel Havemann, *Congress and the Budget* (Bloomington: Indiana University Press, 1978), p. 22.

22. *Cong. Rec.*, March 22, 1967, p. 7631.

Congress had all but unanimously supported in previous legislation and over which the Appropriations Committee had little or no control. They defended increases in the number of Post Office employees on the grounds that the volume of mail was growing. Supporters of the bill focused attention on the details, explaining that overall increases inevitably followed justifiable and congressionally sanctioned increases in the components.

Through this period many members of Congress were deeply dissatisfied by the overall size of the budget, but they were incapable of bringing this dissatisfaction to bear upon particular items in the budget. There was no procedural impediment to prevent opponents of government growth from seeking to curtail expenditures by systematically proposing reductions in programs they thought bloated. This strategy was not pursued, however, undoubtedly because its success was thought unlikely. Proposals to cut specific programs generate specific opposition, but proposals to cut the total do not because they attack nothing in particular. Efforts to recommit appropriations bills, even when they did not pass, gained substantial support because they did not threaten any individual programs. Efforts to cut particular items in appropriations bills were not particularly effective and reduced spending far less than the recommittal motions.

This means of reducing spending, blind to policy consequences, saved several billion dollars—far more than the savings through the more orthodox approach of cutting specified programs by fixed amounts. In 1967, twenty-three amendments proposing specific reductions from the regular appropriations bills were voted upon in the House, and of these seven won. Two of the

seven did not save money directly; the other five successful amendments cut: (1) $10 million from rent supple-
ments; (2) $19 million in interest from participation
sales certificates; (3) $1.7 million from the Lincoln-
Dickey School power project in Maine; (4) $300,000 by
eliminating fifteen positions from the office of the Treasury secretary; (5) $2.2 million from Post Office admin-
istrative costs. According to my estimate, floor amendments reduced appropriations for FY 1968 by $33.2
million in a year when spending rose by a total of $20.6
billion.[23] It should be obvious that efforts to control
spending growth by means of this type of amendment
would accomplish little. On the other hand, by ordering
the executive branch to cut two appropriations bills by
5 percent, much larger amounts were saved with far less
effort.

Spending Ceilings

Efforts in 1966 and 1967 to reduce individual appropriations bills achieved a relatively meager degree of success and were discontinued thereafter. However, from
1967 onward there was a series of efforts, many successful, to enact binding spending ceilings. Such ceilings
took various forms, but typically they set a maximum
level of outlays in a fiscal year and directed the president to allocate spending cuts sufficient to maintain the
ceiling. Democrats on the Appropriations Committee
consistently opposed reductions by this means—just as
they also opposed reductions of appropriations bills—
but the Ways and Means Committee often supported
them. Frequently Republicans proposed expenditure

23. Information on appropriations amendments was compiled
from *CQ Almanac, 1967*.

ceilings as floor amendments to "must" legislation such as debt ceiling bills and continuing resolutions.

Disagreements between the House and the Senate in 1967 over the appropriations reductions adopted by the House led to a protracted stalemate that compelled the adoption of several continuing resolutions. These became the vehicle for several Republican attempts to impose an overall spending ceiling. Frank Bow first sought to impose the ceiling in the Appropriations Committee, proposing that FY 1968 spending be held to $131.5 billion, some $5 billion below administration estimates. *Congressional Quarterly* reported that "the Bow amendment was described as 'unusual' by an Appropriations Committee spokesman. Capitol Hill observers could recall no previous occasion on which the Appropriations Committee had formally considered a proposal to limit federal expenditures" as opposed to cutting individual programs.[24] Bow lost in committee, but his idea had many lives. When the continuing resolution to which he had originally tried to attach his proposal came to the floor, he moved to recommit for the purpose of attaching the $131.5 billion spending limit. As he had in debate over reductions of appropriations bills, Bow did not attempt to explain how the money might or ought to be saved. He argued simply that $131.5 billion was a lot of money and ought to suffice to run the government: "As I say, Mr. Speaker, the estimate of expenditures was $125 billion last year. Why cannot we go with $131 billion?"[25] The motion passed, 202–182. When the continuing resolution returned to the floor on October 3 the spending limitation was again debated, but this time it lost narrowly. Congress had to pass another continuing resolu-

24. Ibid., p. 662.
25. *Cong. Rec.*, Sept. 27, 1967, p. 26958.

tion on October 10, and the tenacious Mr. Bow proposed his amendment yet again, and won. It ultimately became law, yielding savings estimated by OMB at $4 billion.[26]

Yet, through other almost simultaneous actions, Congress undermined its apparent resolve to cut spending and showed that alterations in the way issues were framed could elicit startlingly different expressions of budgetary preference. Inconsistent congressional action on the budget was displayed most glaringly in the behavior of the House on a Labor-HEW conference report in 1967. On October 3, the House had been locked in an acrimonious dispute over the Republican proposal to amend a continuing resolution to authorize the president to cut it by $4 billion. On that day the effort was narrowly defeated, but not before its supporters uttered many dark words about the evil consequences that would follow if Congress did not reduce federal spending. Mr. John Byrnes (R-Wis.) of the Ways and Means Committee declared, "Yes, this may be the most important vote of this session of Congress. To be decided by this vote is whether or not the House of Representatives will face up to the opportunity to do something about the dangerous deficit facing us. I would warn that you turn it down at your peril."[27] The Appropriations Committee was criticized for its lack of economy, as were members of the Democratic party more generally.

George Mahon, chairman of the Appropriations Committee, did not dispute the need for reductions, but he urged the House not to give away its power. He maintained that the normal appropriations process was adequate to achieve savings. If Congress wished to reduce

26. *CQ Almanac, 1967*, pp. 660–670.
27. *Cong. Rec.*, Oct. 3, 1967, p. 27649.

spending, then it should cut programs; he informed his colleagues that they would have such an opportunity to curb spending when considering a $13 billion Labor-HEW conference report the following day. "If the House feels that the amounts agreed to are excessive," he explained, "the conference report is subject to recommittal."[28]

Judging from the close vote on the expenditure limitation, which was killed by a vote of 213–205, and by the strong opinions expressed that day, one would have thought that the House was in the midst of a full-fledged battle over spending restraint. The next day, however, when the Labor-HEW conference report appeared on the House floor just as Mahon promised, the mood of the House seemed completely transformed. Members of the conference committee of both parties began their usual love feast, praising each other and the bill—which they all agreed was very economical. Melvin Laird, a leader of the economy drive and supporter of the Bow cutback proposal, heaped praise upon Daniel Flood (D-Pa.), who had led the House side in the conference and who, according to Laird, had extracted numerous concessions from the Senate conferees. Robert Michel also lauded Flood, who responded: "I am most grateful to the gentleman from Illinois. . . . I am only sorry that Mrs. Flood is not in the gallery to hear that accolade." Michel promised to send her a copy of that day's *Record*.[29] Flood said he could see no reason why the bill should not pass unanimously, and at first no member rose to disagree. The previous day's ardor for economy seemed to have cooled considerably; it was replaced by the usual consensual appropriations politics.

Only Representative H. R. Gross (R-Iowa), who made

28. Ibid.
29. *Cong. Rec.*, Oct. 4, 1967, p. 27734.

a practice of objecting to every appropriations bill, generally on the most trivial grounds, spoke against the bill. In this case, he inquired whether there was in the bill any money for "so-called rat extermination." Flood said that a very small amount was included for that purpose; then he thanked Gross for his contribution to the debate, "I would have been disappointed if my friend from Iowa had not risen to the occasion. He always does."[30] But apart from the lonely foray of Mr. Gross,[31] which received no support, one would have thought that Flood's prediction of quick and easy passage was entirely correct. Somehow, a $13 billion Labor-HEW bill that represented a $259 million increase over the previous year did not evoke the same antispending sentiments that the unspecified cut did the day before. Evidently the opposition to big spending appeared only when Congress considered vague cuts or discussed the total.

Then George Mahon delivered a speech that was bizarre by congressional standards and shattered the consensus. Normally we do not expect floor debate to have a crucial impact on legislation, nor do we expect chairs to undermine bills from their own committees. But in this case Mahon's speech led directly to the bill's recommittal. "Mr. Speaker," he began:

> I find myself quite bruised from the economy battle of recent days. When I recall that this conference report calls for $13.2 billion, and I look about me

30. Ibid., p. 27731.
31. The long career of Representative Gross saw many lonely forays. His obituary reported that "Mr. Gross often began his speeches with the question, 'How much will this boondoggle cost?' He once startled his colleagues on the House floor by questioning the use of Federal funds to pay for the gas consumed by the eternal flame on the grave of John F. Kennedy." *New York Times*, Sept. 24, 1987, p. 49. In addition, see Fenno, *Power of the Purse*, pp. 447–448, for a discussion of Appropriations Committee reactions to Mr. Gross.

and see so few members on the floor, I am inclined to ask, "Where are the economy warriors of yesterday?" . . .

I speak with feeling about this matter because I am supposed to be the leader in bringing in a bill rescinding appropriations, not increasing them. How can I bring in a resolution to rescind if I do not have the recision troops? I need to know, really, whether the economy drive is skindeep or bonedeep.

Mahon listed possible objections to the conference report. It was, he said, in thirteen instances higher than the president's recommendation (yet still below the president's budget in total), in twenty-nine instances above the original House-passed bill, and in sixty-six instances above the 1966 appropriation. Mahon taunted the Republicans who yesterday supported cuts but today raised no objection to the conference report.

We are moving forward and upward on a very broad scale, I would say. I would remark, in calmness, that this is escalation, not recision, my colleagues. Where and when does the minority propose that we begin to cut to achieve the $5 billion non-defense expenditure cut, which, as we have pointed out repeatedly, will require appropriations cuts in the total sum of perhaps $10 billion? Does the minority propose that tomorrow we rescind the increases that we approve today? I hold my hands aloft and say, Mr. Speaker, what direction? What direction?

Mahon's speech left members on the House floor stunned and Republicans embarrassed. Mahon was asked if he was now opposing the bill; he said he was not. A particularly bewildered Melvin Laird said: "I would like to say to the gentleman from Texas that your speech here today has undercut the conference committee more than any speech I have ever heard on the floor of the House."[32] Indeed it did undercut the bill, which only moments before seemed destined to pass routinely. Frank Bow quickly announced that he would move to recommit the bill to conference for the purpose of cutting all increases above the president's request, for a saving of about $20 million.

Mahon's purpose was not to kill the bill but probably to encourage a greater degree of consistency. Inconsistency—strident calls for cuts in the abstract combined with an unwillingness to reduce individual programs—made the position of the Appropriations Committee virtually untenable, as Mahon explained in his speech. His speech successfully evoked the dormant spirit of economy. Apparently prodding of this sort was required to force members of the House to connect their preference for less overall spending with a particular bill. But once the economy mood was evoked, it superceded all other considerations. Laird and Flood both attempted to convince their colleagues that the $20 million now proposed for elimination should not be cut. It would come from the National Institutes of Health, educational assistance for the handicapped, and Gallaudet College, a school for the deaf. Their defense of the increases was unsuccessful, although no one suggested that these programs particularly deserved to be cut. Under ordinary circumstances these programs would have enjoyed strong bipartisan support, but the resurgence of the previous enthusiasm for budget cutting displaced all thought about the programs and their merits. The prob-

32. *Cong. Rec.*, Oct. 4, 1967, p. 27736.

lem was that they were over the president's budget at a time when the economy mood struck. Bow's motion passed by a comfortable margin of 226–174.[33]

Efforts to cut spending by enacting ceilings on outlays continued. In 1968, Congress enacted a $180.1 billion spending ceiling, about $6 billion less than outlays would otherwise have been. John Williams (R-Dela.) originated the spending ceiling in the Senate as a floor amendment to a bill levying a tax surcharge. The $6 billion in reductions was to be allocated by the administration. Like previous efforts to reduce outlays, this was completely general, criticizing the total but no particular program. Again in 1969 and 1970 Congress adopted expenditure ceilings.[34] In these years, Congress resolved its budgetary problems by standing in favor of lower overall spending, refused to cut programs, and punted the issue to the executive branch.

In 1972 the budgetary situation reached a crisis when President Nixon harshly criticized congressional handling of the budget, denounced budgetary procedures in Congress, and demanded that Congress grant him the authority to cut spending in order to maintain a $250 billion spending ceiling. Congress agreed with the president that spending was too high, despite every single member of Congress having voted for at least some spending increases that allowed overall spending to rise to unacceptable levels. In 1972 Congress passed a dazzling array of spending increases, most by huge majorities, and a substantial number unanimously. Efforts to reduce their magnitude failed.

Congress passed a 20 percent increase in Social Security benefits; both chambers rejected amendments to

33. Ibid., p. 27737, vote #296.
34. *CQ Almanac, 1969*, pp. 193–200.

hold the increase to only 10 percent. The largest Defense and Labor-HEW appropriations bills in history passed, and efforts to reduce them failed. Railroad retirements were increased to keep pace with Social Security. Veterans' benefits were increased. Revenue sharing, costing $30 billion over five years, was adopted. A $18 billion water pollution control bill was enacted over a presidential veto. Democrats and Republicans alike supported these increases. Judging by its actions on individual bills, Congress solidly favored bigger and more expensive government. Hostility to big government existed only at the level of the abstract; it did not extend to decisions on real programs.

In a message on July 26, 1972, President Nixon called for a spending ceiling; he insisted that, since Congress would not restrain spending, he should be granted unrestricted authority to cut spending. A protracted battle followed and continued through many skirmishes until the end of the session. Many members of Congress agreed with the president that there was a problem, but there was less agreement on exactly what ought to be done. In the Senate, William Roth (R-Dela.) offered an amendment to a bill increasing the debt ceiling. His amendment proposed setting a $246.5 billion spending ceiling. It passed, but this show of toughness was almost immediately softened when the Senate passed two more amendments, each of which weakened the ceiling. The ceiling remains were removed in conference committee.

In October the debt ceiling had to be raised once more, giving Nixon another opportunity to extract the spending ceiling from Congress. In a national radio address on October 7 he berated Congress for its irresponsibility and claimed that failure to adopt the ceiling would force a tax increase. Members of Congress did not dispute the necessity of cuts, but there was a spirited discussion of means. Opponents of the spending ceiling claimed it abdicated legislative power to the executive branch.

The Ways and Means Committee reported a debt ceiling bill that included a spending ceiling in conformity with Nixon's request. Hoping to blunt this attack on the Appropriations Committee jurisdiction, George Mahon attempted to pass an amendment that would require Nixon to submit to Congress a proposed set of reductions. True to the ethos of his committee, Mahon tried to fix attention on the components of the budget. His amendment, supported by the Democratic leadership of the House, failed, 167–216—only eight Republicans voted for it, and sixty Democrats were opposed.[35] The House was clearly on record in favor of reductions by the president.

Like Ways and Means, the Senate Finance Committee reported a debt ceiling bill that provided a spending ceiling and authorized the president to make cuts. On the floor Len Jordan (R-Idaho) offered an amendment to require the president to cut all programs by the same percentage; it passed, 46–28. Having thus limited the president's authority to cut, the Senate passed the bill, 61–11.[36] The Senate supported reductions but preferred a less sweeping grant of power to the president.

Ultimately the debt ceiling bill passed Congress (as it must), but in the closing hours of the legislative session the expenditure limitation was deleted due to the House and Senate's inability to resolve their disagreement over the amount of presidential discretion. The failure of the

35. *CQ Almanac, 1972*, p. 420.
36. Ibid., p. 422.

ceiling to become law does not diminish the fact that majorities in both chambers did support the ceiling, just as they had done in previous years.

After the failure of the expenditure ceiling to pass, Nixon immediately vetoed a clean water public works bill that authorized $18 billion in projects. Congress overrode the veto the next day, providing yet another splendid example of inconsistent congressional behavior. Although they had been locked in battle over the problem of reducing spending, which was universally held to be too large, this concern was not brought to bear upon individual spending bills.

By 1972 Congress had enacted spending ceilings for five consecutive years, granting the president extraordinary authority over spending. When Congress did not enact a ceiling in 1972, President Nixon arrogated to himself the power Congress denied him and began to withhold appropriated spending. Almost immediately after congressional failure to adopt a ceiling in December 1972, the Nixon administration announced a series of impoundments. The administration reasoned that legislation *authorized* agencies to spend money but did not *require* that money be spent, and so it was within the discretion of the executive branch not to spend money and even to terminate entire programs.[37] Court decisions did not support the Nixon administration's interpretation of executive authority and compelled the release of impounded funds. This was of course a victory for Congress, but it did not lessen the widely perceived need to reform congressional procedures for handling the budget.

The budget battles of 1972 were the most acrimonious

37. Fisher, *Presidential Spending Power*, pp. 176–177.

and protracted of this period, and they left no one satisfied. Congress had shown everyone that it was incapable of handling the budget. The House Appropriations Committee, the traditional guardian of the Treasury, came under severe and unaccustomed attack for being overly loose with public money. Democrats and Republicans were at odds over spending ceilings, with Republicans almost unanimously supporting the ceilings but still supporting individual programs. Conflict with the president was especially severe. Congressional incapacity with respect to the budget, combined with Nixon's enthusiasm in challenging Congress, threatened to reduce congressional power enormously in the budget. In response to this crisis, the Ways and Means Committee proposed in the debt ceiling bill of October 1972 that a temporary committee be formed to investigate possible reforms of congressional budget procedure. This committee was formed, and its recommendations became the basis for the Budget Act of 1974 (discussed in detail in Chapter 2).

Is Congressional Behavior Rational?

Simple logic and rationality would seem to require that when members of Congress vote for a large number of spending increases in particular programs and vote against reductions in programs, they should not vote for restrictive spending ceilings. In the period of 1966–1972, at least, neither Congress as a whole nor many of its members adhered to this conception of rational behavior. Inconsistent behavior resulted, because of the contradictory nature of member preferences, an array of political pressures that did not reward consistency, and fragmented budgetary processes that did not in any way encourage members to resolve conflicts between their preferences on the parts and the whole.

If we consider rationality of preference and choice to consist primarily of consistency and coherence, then the behavior of many members of Congress was clearly irrational in this period. But the irrationality disappears if we view member behavior through the lens of electoral concerns. Given the desire of members to curry favor with their constituents for reelection and the existence of a budgetary procedure that discouraged consistency, it made perfect sense for a representative to vote for spending increases for particular programs, claiming credit for these, and then to vote for an overall spending ceiling, lending credence to his position-taking against "runaway government spending." The blatant hypocrisy of a legislator attacking the big government he helped to create did not prevent him from gaining reelection.

Contradictory behavior on the budget is encouraged by asymmetries of political pressure. There are constituencies for higher spending on particular programs, and there are constituencies that clamor for lower overall spending. But there are fewer constituencies that lobby against spending on particular programs. Thus a largely unopposed pressure for more spending on programs coexists with a pressure for lower overall spending. There is no lobby for consistency per se. Senator Kent Conrad (D-N.D.) explains: "Hundreds of people come to me each month who want more money. Dozens come by and want lower taxes. But no one ever comes up to me about the big picture."[38] To vote against a particular program is to vote in most cases against an iden-

38. *New York Times,* April 20, 1989, p. 7.

tifiable constituency. Voting to cut a program makes enemies, and enemies have long memories. Moreover, the savings that accrue from any one cut are so small— even trivial in the context of total spending—that no constituency will take favorable notice of votes to cut. Members of Congress seek to cultivate friends, not enemies, so it should scarcely be surprising that few want to vote for specific reductions. Charles Schultze contends that a guiding principle in American politics is "do no direct harm."[39] Specific cuts inflict a direct harm and are thus to be avoided.

Spending ceilings enforced by the president are more popular because they do not require a representative to vote against any particular constituency. In making cuts in this period, Congress consistently shifted the onus of cutting programs to that convenient scapegoat—the executive branch. In 1967, Congress voted to authorize President Johnson to cut spending, even though that was a power he had not sought and a responsibility he wished to avoid. Johnson argued that if Congress was dissatisfied with the level of spending, it should make the cuts and take the blame.[40] Votes in favor of spending ceilings are relatively safe, but votes against ceilings are not, for they are often highly visible, important votes that are unambiguously associated with austerity—a goal few members of Congress wish to oppose in so public a way.[41]

There are, of course, some exceptions to this "logic of spending reductions." Some programs have no voting

39. Charles Schultze, *The Public Use of Private Interest* (Washington, D.C.: Brookings Institution, 1977), pp. 70–72.

40. *CQ Almanac, 1967*, p. 663.

41. For an analysis of efforts of politicians to shift blame to others, see Kent Weaver, "The Politics of Blame Avoidance," *Journal of Public Policy* 6 (Oct.–Nov. 1986): 371–398.

constituency, and others have weak ones, inviting attacks. Economy moods in Congress consequently wreak great havoc with foreign aid appropriations, which Congress cuts with enthusiasm. In 1967 Congress was able to cut $10 million in rent supplements from the Independent Offices-HUD appropriations because, according to *Congressional Quarterly*, there was no significant organized interest lobbying for their retention. Urban renewal survived a similar assault because mayors mobilized in its defense.[42]

A fragmented budget procedure facilitates reelection by enabling members to claim credit for that which is popular and avoid blame for that which is not. It permits members to vote for programs, gaining the support of those who benefit, and then to vote against the aggregate consequences of their actions on the parts of the budget. Moreover, fragmentation permits obfuscation and erects barriers behind which legislators can hide, making it difficult for constituents to evaluate their representative's overall performance. In taking advantage of fragmentation, electorally motivated members may behave inconsistently, but from the standpoint of electoral theories, there is nothing irrational about such inconsistencies.

Choosing Procedures

In choosing how to pose budgetary issues, members of Congress also decide to which political pressures they will expose themselves. Procedures that stress the consideration of individual components of the budget expose members primarily to pressure from groups with a

42. *CQ Almanac, 1967,* p. 469.

direct stake in programs and tend to diffuse the influence of broader publics. Consideration of more general
policy questions, such as the total and the size of the deficit, invite the participation of broader interests and
tend to blunt the effectiveness of narrower groups.

Representatives evidently understood the importance
of "framing" an issue and skillfully employed what William Riker has termed "heresthetics" to manipulate
congressional behavior. Proponents of spending reductions sought to frame amendments to reduce spending
in the most general possible fashion while the defenders
of programs sought to secure increases in their programs by means of floor amendments increasing appropriations. Individual members, in taking the path of
least resistance, voted in utterly contradictory ways.
They produced an insane budget policy, but they
achieved reelection with great regularity.

If it were actually the case that members of Congress
were concerned solely with reelection and that they subordinated all policy decisions to the electoral goal, then
it would seem that they should find the chaos caused by
their behavior untroubling. As Mayhew and Fenno have
both explained, unpopular aggregate policy consequences do not pose problems for individual members,
who are responsible only for their own votes and able to
distinguish themselves from the overall reputation of
Congress. Electoral challengers cannot effectively use
the poor reputation of Congress as a whole against a
single incumbent who, in any case, is probably running
for Congress by running against it.[43]

In fact, large numbers of senators and representatives
were deeply dissatisfied with congressional policy mak-

43. See Richard Fenno, *Homestyle: House Members in Their Districts* (Boston: Little, Brown, 1978), pp. 162–168.

ing, and they expressed their displeasure by voting to establish a study committee to recommend budgetary reform. One might easily imagine that the call for a study commission was purely symbolic, intended only to diffuse presidential criticism of Congress. Two years later, however, Congress adopted a new budget process, replacing a process nearly ideal for electoral purposes with one that would require voting on the size of the budget and the deficit; this adoption greatly integrated budgetary decision making.

To understand this behavior we must presume that members of Congress do in fact care about more than simply being reelected. My view, supported by the events leading to the adoption of the Congressional Budget Act, is that members of Congress are subject to multiple, conflicting concerns. They do most certainly care about reelection, and for that reason, if for no other, they care deeply about serving the needs of their constituents. But they do not subordinate all other concerns to the goal of reelection.

Judging by congressional behavior one might well think that individual members were guided solely or largely by electoral concerns and scarcely at all by a desire to produce a sensible budget. If members did desire to produce a good budget, they must have found that voting responsibly conflicted sharply with electoral concerns. Faced with a choice between a defensible budget and reelection pressures, many succumbed to the electoral connection. However, when members find that the structure of congressional procedure drives them consistently to vote against their preferences or to adopt absurd positions, they can and do change procedure in order to reduce the tension between policy and electoral concerns. One can view the budget process they adopted in 1974 as an effort to enable themselves to enact a coherent budget without putting themselves excessively at political risk. From their votes, we can infer the preferences of individual representatives. But when choice is influenced by procedure, as it surely is in Congress, choices may not indicate underlying preferences fully or accurately. Under such circumstances, choice of procedure may better indicate true preference. From their contradictions over the budget, we can conclude that members of Congress care a lot about reelection. From their decision to change congressional procedure, we can deduce that members of Congress care about reelection and policy and seek to balance these two goals.

2

A New Budget Process

In the closing days of the disastrous 1972 legislative session, the House of Representatives debated a bill to raise the debt ceiling and impose a federal spending limit for the year. George Mahon, the beleaguered chairman of the Appropriations Committee, rose to criticize the chairman of Ways and Means, Wilbur Mills, whose committee had written the bill. In unusually direct language he accused Mills of hypocrisy for leading the charge to impose a spending ceiling after sponsoring legislation that provided large spending increases.

It surprises me a bit that my good friend from Arkansas would speak so fervently about economy and a balanced budget when he has led the fight to bring about the condition with which we are confronted today.

Why would he point the finger at the Appropriations Committee with respect to the problem of expenditures when the gentleman led the fight for the

$30 billion Revenue Sharing which to a very large extent brought us to this moment of distress.

The President tried to keep us from providing a 20-percent increase in Social Security, but he was overridden with the help of the economy minded chairman of the Committee on Ways and Means.

Mills's reply to these comments illustrates perfectly the problem with congressional budgetary procedures. Mahon had sought to frame his dispute around the question of consistency, but Mills evaded that issue altogether by implying that Mahon was simply opposed to spending on those particular programs. Mills announced, "Mr. Chairman, I want to publicly apologize to the gentleman from Texas for having aroused his ire on the Social Security bill which we passed in the House. I am sorry he is not in agreement on that."[1]

This was pure sophistry on the part of Mills. Mahon had not questioned the Social Security increase, only the apparent contradictions in Mills's behavior. Nonetheless, once Mills suggested that Mahon was opposed to Social Security increases, Mahon was forced to beat a hasty retreat and explain that he believed the increases to be justified. Mills used the same ploy to defend revenue sharing. "If the gentleman is opposed to that program," he continued, "he will have a chance to vote against it, and maybe the House wants to kill it."[2] In this exchange Mills took advantage of the decision structure of Congress to direct attention from the rather abstract question of budgetary consistency to the more concrete desirability of Social Security and revenue sharing. He

1. *Cong. Rec.*, Oct. 10, 1972, p. 34599.
2. Ibid.

was, moreover, successful: the House voted for the spending ceiling, which was attached to a debt ceiling bill, and then voted for revenue sharing.

Somewhat ironically, one provision of the spending ceiling bill established a special joint congressional committee to study ways of reforming congressional procedure. The committee recommended replacing sequential consideration of spending and revenue legislation with a simultaneous consideration that would both encourage the kind of comprehensive consideration Mahon had sought and discourage the artful dodging Mills employed.

The structure of congressional budgeting from 1966 to 1974 almost guaranteed that members of Congress, in the course of attending to their electoral concerns, would enact inconsistent policy. We can see their 1974 reforms as efforts to establish a budget system that would enable them to (1) enact a sane and sensible budget policy, (2) escape reliance on the executive branch in so doing, and (3) avoid losing their office. Acting to commit themselves to a comprehensive, all-inclusive budget process hardly seems like the behavior of a legislator interested only in achieving reelection by distributing benefits to constituents. The goal of reelection is certainly very much on their minds; nonetheless, many of them apparently also care about enacting good public policy. More specifically, they want to be able to enact good public policy without endangering their reelection. When the two goals come into conflict, as they often do, most sensible members will do the politically expedient thing.

Under Congress's traditional budget system, the course of action for a sensible, electorally motivated legislator on a bill to increase a popular program was rather obvious. He should support it because there is political gain in doing so and none for opposing it. How should he vote on an amendment to reduce a program? Obviously, he should oppose it for the same reason. What about a bill to establish a binding ceiling on federal outlays? Clearly he should not oppose it, for to do so would invite a political opponent to claim that he had voted for bigger spending and deficits. A member of Congress following the line of least resistance on a series of such votes would produce a string of contradictory votes, and the presence of a number of others in Congress doing the same would cause Congress itself to make contradictory decisions. And that, in fact, is what happened in Congress between 1966 and 1974. In the near term the actions of Congress are determined by the decision structure and the ways members manipulate its structure. But over time legislators can alter those procedures if they are seen to distort systematically the expressions of the will of Congress.

By changing the way in which procedure frames budgetary issues, members of Congress can manipulate the array of political pressures that will bear on their choices, and in this way they may manipulate actual budgetary choices. Under a fragmented budgetary procedure, members of Congress faced alternating pressures, first to spend and then not to spend, depending on whether the particular issue before them highlighted the total or the parts. By replacing their fragmented procedure with a more integrated one, they created a situation in which they were exposed to both kinds of pressure simultaneously. When Congress must vote on the entire budget at once—considering the total amount of spending, revenue, and deficit, as well as a distribution of that spending—pressures to spend presumably will be arrayed against pressures not to raise the total or run a deficit. Whether this should result in more spending or less is a matter of conjecture (and will be discussed later in this chapter). But regardless of the policy consequences that attend increased integration of budgeting, we should expect that individuals, and Congress, will be able to act more consistently than possible with a fragmented procedure.

The Joint Committee Report

Upon enactment of the debt ceiling bill in October 1972, a Joint Study Committee on Budget Control was formed; its members were drawn almost exclusively from the Appropriations and Ways and Means Committees in the House and Appropriations and Finance Committees in the Senate. By February 1973 the study committee had already issued an interim report in which it analyzed the problems with the existing congressional procedure. In April it issued its final recommendations. "The present institutional arrangements," the committee wrote,

> in many cases appear to make it impossible to decide between competing priorities. . . . The fact that no committee has the responsibility to decide whether or not total outlays are appropriate in view of the current situation appears to be responsible for much of the problem. Perhaps still more critical for the process is the distribution of jurisdictions [over spending] among several different committees. As a result each spending bill tends to

be considered by Congress as a separate entity, and any assessment of relative priorities among spending programs is made solely within the context of the bill then before Congress.[3]

The committee identified a number of features of congressional procedure as culpable. In its interim report, the committee argued that because of the absence of an overall budgetary vote, Congress "does not examine extensively the whole budget with the purpose of passing judgment on whether the totals are satisfactory or whether the relationship of the various parts, one to another, is satisfactory."[4]

The interim report recommended creating a mechanism to allow Congress to determine proper levels of expenditure, revenue, and deficit. It made several suggestions: (1) Congress should be equipped to choose relative budget priorities and possible budget reductions; (2) the budget process should be comprehensive, covering all types of spending; (3) there should be a means for allocating shares of total spending to committees; (4) spending ceilings must be binding and enforceable; (5) permanent committees on the budget should be established to oversee the budget process. Overall these recommendations gave members of Congress the ability to decide on a total, relate that total to programs in the budget, and enforce their decisions. This would reduce the extent to which the budget merely "happened" and at least

3. Joint Study Committee on Budget Control, *Recommendations for Improving Congressional Control Over Budgetary Outlay and Receipt Totals*, H. Rept. 93–147, 93rd Cong., 1st sess. (USGPO, 1973), p. 1.

4. Joint Study Committee on Budget Control, *Improving Congressional Control Over Budgetary Outlay and Receipt Totals*, H. Rept. 93–13, 93rd Cong., 1st sess. (USGPO, 1973), p. 6.

partly transform a budgetary process that had been almost exclusively "bottom-up" into one that was, to a greater extent, "top-down."

In 1974 both Houses of Congress voted overwhelmingly in favor of the Budget and Impoundment Control Act. President Nixon signed it shortly before resigning from office, and Congress thus provided itself with a regularized budget process for the first time. The Budget Act, consistent with the aims and goals laid out in both the interim report and the final report of the joint study committee, established procedures for comprehensively considering budgetary issues and for deciding on aggregate figures on expenditures, revenues, and the deficit. In various ways, the Budget Act also provided for procedures to ensure that decisions regarding the aggregate budget be implemented. This is the stickiest part of the budget process. Perhaps most important for some members were the act's provisions to limit presidential ability to impound funds appropriated by Congress.

The goals laid out by the joint study committee could not possibly be achieved without disturbing the previous distribution of power, particularly the power and independence of the taxing and spending committees. As could be expected, these committees ensured that the final recommendations and the Budget Act itself did not intrude too deeply into their traditional prerogatives, and consequently the act itself was weakened in several respects while being considered. The Budget Act was particularly inadequate in the areas of enforcement and comprehensiveness. But in subsequent years, Congress has moved quite consistently, if not rapidly, toward comprehensiveness and enforceability and toward greater compliance with the principle that the budget should be the result of specific and conscious decision rather than a compilation of separate legislative actions.

Budget Resolutions

Very generally, the budget process is a mechanism by which Congress can adopt an overall statement of budget policy and a series of devices by which those decisions can be translated into actual policy. The central and most notable innovation of the process is the budget resolution, a comprehensive statement of the general outlines of the budget; it is intended to be adopted early in the session, before floor consideration of actual spending and revenue legislation, and designed to structure subsequent legislative action.

Budget resolutions consist of (1) aggregate target figures for revenue, expenditure, and the total amount of federal debt; (2) a breakdown of spending into nineteen functional categories, such as national defense, social security, interest, health, and education; and (3) enforcement procedures. The budget resolution thus addresses the most often repeated criticism of the previous budgetary arrangements, which was that Congress had no opportunity to consider the whole budget. The budget resolution enables members to view comprehensively budget policy, and it also makes it more difficult for individual members to escape blame for the aggregate consequences of congressional action—or at least it does so for members who vote for the resolution.[5]

5. The safest course is to vote against budget resolutions. Rep. Trent Lott (R-Miss.), the minority whip, recommended in 1987 that Republicans oppose the resolution on the grounds that "you do not ever get into trouble for those budgets which you vote against. It is

The budget resolution, because it requires simultaneous consideration of all budgetary issues, holds out the possibility of eliminating the contradictory behavior that made such a mess of congressional budgeting in the 1960s and early 1970s. Sequential consideration of budgetary issues allows the expression of first one preference and then the expression of another quite contradictory preference, without in any way resolving the conflict. When voting on a budget resolution, it becomes much harder to avoid making choices. One cannot vote for large spending increases, reduced taxes, and a low deficit (unless one either violates mathematical consistency or uses incorrect estimates of expenditures and revenues). Ideally, a legislator will be forced to weigh his conflicting budgetary preferences against each other in voting on the budget resolution.

Budget resolutions and appropriations bills represent fundamentally different approaches to budget control. Resolutions are pitched at an extremely high level of generality, ignoring all amounts smaller than $100 million on the grounds that the resolutions deal only with the broad outlines of policy, not the details. Many details, of course, may be hidden within $100 million. Nonetheless, members still try to use the resolution as a means of establishing a congressional commitment to specific programs, even for amounts much less than

---

the ones that you vote for that get you in trouble." Thomas Foley (D-Wash.), the majority leader, reacted "passionately" to Lott's advice, according to *Congressional Quarterly.* "Don't vote and you won't get into trouble," he said. "What a motto for leadership. What a motto for carrying out the responsibilities and obligations of membership in this body." *Congressional Quarterly Weekly Report*, April 11, 1987, p. 659; hereafter *CQ Weekly Report.*

$100 million. In 1982, for example, Senator Dale Bumpers (D-Ark.) offered a floor amendment to the budget resolution. The following exchange with Pete Domenici (R-N.M.) ensued:

> MR. DOMENICI: How much does the Senator propose to add to function 550 for the immunization program?
>
> MR. BUMPERS: The figures are $3.7 million for 1983 and $6.2 million in 1984, and $8.7 million in 1985.
>
> MR. DOMENICI: The Senator is not speaking of billions.
>
> MR. BUMPERS: Millions. I know it is difficult for the chairman of the Budget Committee to get used to dealing with millions, but my amendment involves millions.
>
> MR. DOMENICI: It is not difficult for the chairman to understand millions. It is just that it does not show up in the budget, even if we accept the amendment.[6]

Appropriations bills tend toward the opposite extreme, often delving into minute detail about the funding and operation of agencies, commonly allocating amounts measured in tens of thousands of dollars, and less.

The traditional congressional budgeting system, based as it was upon considering program detail and adopting appropriations bills, has been termed "bottom-up" since it began with the consideration of programs and the total was determined by the choices on the parts. Observers sometimes mistakenly claim that the Budget Act of 1974 introduced "top-down" budget-

6. *Cong. Rec.*, daily edition (May 19, 1982), p. S5535.

ing to Congress, meaning a system in which a choice is first made about the overall size of the budget and then the parts are trimmed to fit within it. Certainly budget resolutions introduce a greater element of top-down budgeting than existed before, yet in deciding on a budget resolution members are highly cognizant of the impact of their choices on particular programs.

Adopting budget resolutions involves a simultaneous consideration of both the parts and the whole: it is not a sequential choice of a total and then an allocation of parts within that amount, as in top-down budgeting. In adopting a budget resolution, Congress decides simultaneously on a total and its distribution among broad functional categories. An explanation of how the Senate Budget Committee wrote resolutions in the period before 1981 illustrates the process of choice. Members of the committee met in a markup session and worked through the budget function by function. The chair proposed an amount for, say, defense, and the committee voted. If the chair's proposal did not receive a majority, another member proposed a different amount; they proceeded in this manner until they achieved majority agreement on each function. The same majority need not support all functions. In voting on amounts for functions, members would not act in ignorance because proposed allocations were based upon assumed levels of funding for particular programs. When a member proposed an increase or a decrease in a function, he or she would typically explain, in fairly specific terms, how the increase or decrease might be allocated. These assumptions were not binding in later deliberations, but the Budget Committees of both chambers strongly believe that they "cannot pull numbers out of the sky" and that the decisions they reach should be informed by an understanding of their probable programmatic consequences.[7]

After voting on the functional allocations the committee would almost invariably discover that the sum of the spending they had agreed upon exceeded their desired expenditure total. Their unpleasant choice was recommending: (1) higher revenues; (2) a higher deficit; or (3) lower spending. The committee then began a second round of deliberations on the functions, attempting to reduce them enough to get the total down to an acceptable level. The final product necessarily consisted of a bundle of compromises, in which members would settle for what they considered too little on their favorite programs and too high a total.

Throughout this protracted process, which often involved more than a hundred votes, the members were aware of how their decisions would affect major programs. In voting on resolutions, members can tell roughly the consequences of particular choices, especially for programs of major scale, about which they care most. Reports from the Budget Committees explain the assumptions upon which the choices are based and compare what the committees and the president have proposed for different programs.

The process I have described conforms to neither the top-down nor the bottom-up model because neither the total nor the parts become subordinate to the other. I prefer a different term, "iterative budgeting." It suggests

7. The functional allocation adopted in the budget resolution binds committees other than Appropriations most effectively. The Appropriations Committee receives a large chunk of money, subdivided by function. In practice the committee has been able to shift money between functions, as long as it stays under the overall ceiling. Other committees are less able to shift money around and are bound more by the functional allocation.

a more complex process, a conversation between the parts and the whole in which one's preference on the whole must be shaped by the sum of one's preferences on programs and one's preferences on programs are influenced by understanding their relationship to the whole budget. I would also contend that iterative budgeting is more rational than either top-down or bottom-up systems. Aaron Wildavsky writes, "Changing our conception of what we ought to prefer under the discipline of our limitations as well as the spur of our aspirations is the highest form of learning."[8] By constantly confronting individuals with the inevitable tension between their preferences on the parts and the whole, an iterative process can conceivably encourage such learning, causing individuals to accommodate conflicting preferences.

Budget resolutions are concurrent resolutions that must negotiate the normal legislative process. They originate in the Budget Committees (of which there is one in each chamber, created by the Budget Act), are debated on the floor, possibly amended, and then voted on. Like ordinary bills, budget resolutions are sent to a conference committee to resolve interchamber differences, and the conference report must of course be adopted by both House and Senate. Although the process by which they are considered in Congress is identical to that used for bills, budget resolutions are not bills, and they do not become laws. They neither require a presidential signature nor are subject to a veto. Budget resolutions are exclusively congressional documents that structure and regulate subsequent activity on spending and taxing legislation. Legislation enacted pursuant to a resolution is, of course, subject to all the normal strictures

8. Aaron Wildavsky, *Speaking Truth to Power* (Boston, Mass.: Little, Brown, 1979), p. 39.

that govern enacting a law. If a resolution requires passage of a tax increase, the president cannot veto the resolution but most certainly can veto any tax bill that passes pursuant to the resolution. Because Congress lacks the power to implement a budget policy unilaterally and requires the president's cooperation in passing legislation, the administration is often consulted closely in the course of drafting a resolution, particularly when the president's party controls at least one chamber of Congress. At least in one case—1981—the budget resolution that was finally adopted may actually have been written in the executive branch.

The Budget Act originally called for two resolutions each year: the first, to be passed by May 15 before committees began reporting new spending legislation, set guidelines for that action; the second, to be passed by September 15 before the beginning of the new fiscal year, was intended to be binding. Since 1980, however, through informal innovations the first has become a binding resolution, and the second resolution has passed completely out of use. The Gramm-Rudman-Hollings legislation adopted in December 1985 introduced many changes in the Budget Act, among them abandoning the second resolution, formalizing the switch to a binding first resolution, and advancing the date for its adoption to April 15. Gramm-Rudman-Hollings began as an amendment to a debt ceiling bill in the Senate. Formally known as the Balanced Budget and Deficit Control Act of 1985, it was responsible for the first significant official modifications to the Budget Act. Gramm-Rudman-Hollings altered the timetable of the budget process, requiring both the president's earlier submission of his budget and adoption of the budget resolution earlier in the year. It also formalized the use of reconciliation on the first resolution in the spring and enhanced enforcement procedures.

Enforcement Procedures

Prescribing an expenditure ceiling or an allocation among functions does not in any way ensure their realization in policy. The budget is the product of countless discrete choices embodied in legislation, and for the policy outlined in the resolution to be implemented the legislation that actually governs spending and taxing policy—tax laws, entitlement legislation, and appropriations—must be adjusted to conform with the resolution. This problem of enforcement is the greatest impediment to congressional control of the budget; most significant, the budget process includes practical means of enforcing the choices embodied in the resolution.

The importance of enforcing aggregate decisions at the program level was demonstrated by Representative John Rousselot (R-Calif.) in his quixotic effort to balance the budget in 1982. At the very close of the legislative session that year there was a lull in the floor action as the House waited for the Senate to complete action on a major gas tax and public works bill. The Speaker Pro Tem announced that he would entertain unanimous consent requests to fill up the time. "If anyone wants to say something nice about somebody, this is the time," the Speaker explained, no doubt expecting requests to congratulate championship high school swimming teams, commemorate the birth of triplets, or otherwise immortalize important achievements in the pages of the *Congressional Record*. Without hesitation, John Rousselot asked to be recognized and was. "Mr. Speaker," he said, "I ask unanimous consent that we balance the budget." The Speaker smiled broadly, repeated the request, and then asked if there was any objection. The chamber was silent. Hearing no objection, the Speaker announced that "the request is granted" and banged his gavel.[9] Despite this novel approach to budget control, the budget remained unbalanced. Only by voting smaller appropriations, higher taxes, or reduced entitlements will a deficit be eliminated. Only a budget process that somehow manages to bridge choices on the total and the parts can work.

The enforcement mechanisms of the 1974 Budget Act are not perfect, but neither are the decisions incorporated in the budget resolutions vacuous statements of what Congress would like in the best of all possible worlds. Effectively coordinating choices on the whole and the parts makes the budget process immensely complex. The very simple and quite useless 1946 reform consisted of a few sentences tacked on to a larger committee reform bill mostly as an afterthought. By contrast the 1974 act, running fifty-eight pages, is so intricate that most members of Congress probably only vaguely understand how it works. The complexity is designed not to confuse but to give Congress an ability to control all types of spending. For every different funding mechanism, there must be a means of coordinating it with the overall policy outlined in the resolution. Funding government programs only by means of annual appropria-

9. This landmark in the annals of Congress may be found in the *Cong. Rec.*, daily edition (Dec. 21, 1982), p. H10711. My account differs very slightly from that contained in the *Congressional Record*. I saw the original event on C-SPAN and am supplementing the official transcript with my own recollection of the incident.

tions would provide a simpler route to budget control, but that would be both a bad policy as well as a political impossibility.[10] To implement budget control Congress must develop a repertoire of responses capable of matching the complexity of spending programs. When first adopted the process was clearly inadequate to exercise this control, but during the intervening years it has moved consistently toward comprehensive coverage.

The logic of the budget process is to centralize only decisions about budgetary aggregates and to leave to the committees more specific decisions about implementing the aggregates. In principle, at least, the budget resolutions determine policy only at the greatest level of generality, and committees retain the discretion to decide, on the basis of their greater expertise, how the money allotted to them should be divided among programs. Discussions in the budget committees often are based on very detailed assumptions about how money will be allocated; but these nonbinding assumptions are used only to enhance the credibility of budget resolutions and to show that they are not fabricated. The committees must necessarily retain a significant measure of authority, yet there must also be ways of regulating their

10. The authors of *Setting National Priorities* addressed this issue in 1975: "In a technical sense, the budget would be more controllable if allocations were changed so that more federal workers were hired, if domestic income transfer programs were converted into more active forms of government involvement, or if both measures were taken. It would be bad social policy to manipulate the budget in this manner merely to achieve greater technical controllability, and it would be equally bad to shy away from needed programs because they are classed as uncontrollable. In fact, the technical definition of controllability does not, by itself, provide a sensible guide to government policy." Barry Blechman, Edward Gramlich, and Robert Hartman, *Setting National Priorities: The 1976 Budget* (Washington, D.C.: Brookings Institution, 1975), pp. 196–197.

activity and ensuring that the bills they produce are within the budget. This also promotes the complexity of the process.

As first passed in each chamber, the budget resolution divides total spending into nineteen functional categories. These categories do not correspond to committee jurisdictions but to accounts kept at OMB—a point that causes significant confusion. In certain cases functions will be split among a number of different committees. When voting on the resolution initially in each chamber, members do not know exactly how much each committee will receive, although they have a good idea. The conference report on the budget resolution, however, translates the functional allocations into committee jurisdictions and provides each committee with a total spending ceiling.

Committees then subdivide their total among either subcommittees or programs and report this breakdown back to the budget committees. Thereafter the subdivision is binding upon committee actions, and any legislation they produce in excess of these limits is subject to a point of order. The budget committees have as a primary responsibility the task of tracking bills and informing the House or the Senate whether a particular bill exceeds the amount allocated to that bill or that subcommittee. By this means Congress can ensure that the new legislation it considers neither violates nor contradicts the decision made earlier and included in the budget resolution.

A series of points of order, some adopted in the original Budget Act and others added by Gramm-Rudman, permits Congress to stop budget-busting legislation. That is, when legislation exceeding the amount allowed by the resolution comes to the floor, any member can prevent its consideration by raising a point of order with the presiding officer. Legislation inconsistent with the resolution is then ruled out of order and cannot be passed, but the rules Congress makes it can, in most cases, break. Consequently, "the Budget Act created rules for the Senate [and House] to obey only when and if a majority of its members chose not to set them aside."[11] The 1974 Act permitted the House and the Senate to adopt resolutions to waive rules preventing majorities from doing what they wanted, which was done with some frequency.[12] Gramm-Rudman strengthened the process by requiring a three-fifths majority (the same imposing requirement for invoking cloture) to waive rules enforcing the budget resolution in the Senate. The House can still waive rules with relative ease. But if Congress chooses to exceed its budget resolution, it does so in full knowledge of the consequences of its actions for the budget ceiling.

The points of order can be useful in blocking new legislation, but they do nothing to exert controls over existing entitlement programs, which have contributed most to overall expenditure growth. Entitlements are particularly troublesome from the standpoint of budgetary control because spending on most entitlements goes up with inflation or changes in the economy, even without the passage of new legislation. Initially the budget pro-

11. Stanley Bach, "The Appeal of Order: The Senate's Compliance with its Legislative Rules" (Paper presented at the annual meeting of the Midwestern Political Science Association, April 13–15, 1989, Chicago), p. 1.

12. Richard Cheney and other House Republicans spoke on the House floor for an hour and a half in 1988 to complain of what they considered excessive waivers of Budget Act provisions and other rules. See Richard Cheney, "An Unruly House: A Republican View," *Public Opinion* 11 (Jan./Feb. 1989): 41–44, and *Cong. Rec.*, daily edition (May 24, 1988), pp. H3576–92.

cess introduced no controls of any kind over entitlements, except to curtail the creation of new ones. Earlier versions of the Budget Act had included entitlement controls, but the Ways and Means Committee, with jurisdiction over many of the largest entitlements, was opposed to and successfully fought this intrusion into their domain. The failure of the budget process to include entitlements clearly contradicted the expressed goal of comprehensiveness and caused major problems. Several times early in the life of the act, budget resolutions recommended that entitlements be cut. Absent any enforcement device, the committees with jurisdiction over the programs were able to ignore the resolution and, by their inaction, frustrate the will of the majority as expressed in the resolution.

Reconciliation

The formal language of the Budget Act was not changed, but informal adaptations in using the process helped establish a means of reining in entitlements. In 1980, Democrats in the House and the Senate seized upon a previously disregarded provision of the Budget Act called "reconciliation" and used it to require a number of committees with entitlements to "reconcile" their programs with the overall budget policy. These committees were instructed to produce legislation reducing spending on entitlements in their jurisdictions. Contrary to the predictions of a number of observers, the reconciliation procedure has been used regularly and now constitutes the heart of the budget process. Reconciliation provides for far more intercommittee coordination than was previously possible.

Reconciliation is a two-stage process: it begins with the resolution, including instructions to specific committees to cut entitlement spending or increase revenues; subsequently, instructed committees are to produce legislation implementing the resolution and send it to the budget committee in their chamber. The budget committees bundle all the separate committee-reported reconciliation bills, which are then sent, combined, to the floor for passage. Reconciliation introduces a means of exerting control over existing entitlement programs. Its use has also resulted in the enactment of legislation cutting spending and increasing taxes that would otherwise have been nearly impossible to pass by ordinary legislative procedure.

Interpretations of the Process

The budget process has significantly altered the procedures of Congress, yet its meaning and significance have been the subject of confusion. Many observers contend that the process was enacted for the unambiguous purpose of reducing spending and deficits. After adopting the Budget Act, spending continued to grow and the deficit expanded to almost unbelievable proportions; so these observers hasten to the conclusion that the budget process failed. Louis Fisher, perhaps the most insistent critic of the process, disparages contentions that the process was to be "neutral" toward spending: "It would seem difficult to argue that Congress overhauled its budget process, set up new committees, and created new institutions, such as the Congressional Budget Office, simply to make the process neutral toward spending. The overwhelming motivation was to restrain the growth of federal spending."[13] Elsewhere he writes, "Given the political climate from 1972 to 1974, it seems incongruous to call the Budget Act neutral toward spending."[14] If this interpretation of the act is accepted, then clearly it has been a failure.

An examination of the background of the Budget Act suffices to undermine the view that its clear purpose was to limit spending. The Budget Act passed the Senate by a unanimous vote of 80–0 and the House by a near unanimous 401–6. This alone constitutes strong evidence that, at the time of its passage, the act was not understood to promote spending limitation or any other overtly partisan goal. Certainly, many who voted for it did so hoping that the result would be reduced spending. But it is hard to imagine that the many liberals who voted for the act did so in the belief that spending would be curtailed. Had it been obvious then that the bill had unambiguous implications for spending, the vote would have split along partisan lines.

The legislation setting up the joint study committee charged it with studying "the procedures which should be adopted . . . for establishing and maintaining an overall view of each year's budgetary outlays which is coordinated with an overall view of anticipated revenues for the year." Coordination—not spending restraint—would seem to have been the paramount issue. Similarly, the report of the House Rules Committee accompanying the Budget Act to the floor supports the view that the legislation was not designed to achieve a

13. Louis Fisher, "Ten Years of the Budget Act: Still Searching for Controls," *Public Budgeting & Finance* 5 (Autumn 1985): 14.

14. Louis Fisher, "The Budget Act: A Further Loss of Spending Control," in *Congressional Budgeting: Politics, Process, and Power,* ed. W. Thomas Wander, F. Ted Hebert, and Gary W. Copeland (Baltimore: Johns Hopkins University Press, 1984), p. 172.

particular substantive result, but to provide Congress with better tools for controlling taxing and spending:

> Budget reform and impoundment control have a joint purpose: to restore responsibility for spending policy of the United States to the legislative branch. One without the other would leave Congress in a weak and ineffective position. No matter how prudently Congress discharges its appropriations responsibility, legislative decisions have no meaning if they can be unilaterally abrogated by executive impoundments. On the other hand, if Congress appropriates funds without full awareness of the country's fiscal condition, its actions may be used by the President to justify improper withholding of funds.[15]

The committee report specifically discredits the view that spending reduction was the goal of the legislation when it states that "budget reform must not become an instrument for preventing Congress from expressing its will on spending policy. . . . The constant objective of budget reform must be to make Congress informed about and responsible for its actions, not to take away its power to act."[16]

The budget process was not designed to produce a particular legislative outcome; no particular substantive result is programmed into the legislation. The process does give Congress a greater capacity to cut the budget, but there is nothing to compel Congress to use that process for that purpose. Rather, the process is best understood as an effort to make the budget a matter of

15. House Budget Committee, *Congressional Budget and Impoundment Control Act of 1974—Legislative History*, Committee Print, January 1979, p. 16; hereafter cited *Legislative History*.
16. Ibid., p. 29.

deliberate choice and design, rather than the fortuitous result of noncoordinated, independent committee actions. The purpose of the process is to allow Congress to control the budget—if we understand control to mean the ability of Congress to work its collective will in budgetary policy. This was not possible with the previous arrangements.

Faced with a crisis in the early 1970s, members of Congress could not agree on the direction of federal budget policy, but they could agree on the desirability of diminishing fragmentation. The Budget Act was so extraordinarily popular largely because its provisions pointed to no obvious policy consequence, accommodating multiple, contradictory interpretations. Conservatives hoping for lower spending could support the act, as could liberals who wanted to use it to reassert congressional budgetary power and halt the Nixon impoundments.

Conservatives saw the budget problem as the persistence of large deficits in spite of what seemed like a clear public disapprobation, and they relied on congressional fragmentation to explain this anomaly. The ultimate problems were deficits, but their immediate cause was a budget system that forced members to vote on neither the total nor the deficit. If members voted for towering deficits and then publicly defended those votes, the legislators would either eliminate the deficits or lose their seats—so runs the conservative critique of the former budget process. Paul Craig Roberts, an official in the Reagan Treasury Department, concurs in this procedural, indirect interpretation:

> The Republicans had cooperated in passing the Budget Act of 1974 ... because they thought it

would be used in balancing the budget. Fiscal conservatives thought that their liberal colleagues could too easily legislate big deficits indirectly by voting in favor of many separate appropriations bills. Conservatives believed that if the big spenders had to vote on aggregate expenditure and revenue figures, and thereby on the size of the deficit itself, there would be lower and firmer limits to spending. To their minds, the new budget process was a way to put the big spenders on the spot.[17]

In this view, fragmentation served the purposes of liberals by allowing them to vote for spending increases without also having to vote for tax increases or the ensuing deficit.

Congressional liberals were less concerned by the size of the budget and the deficit, which many regarded as justified by the level of unemployment. They were, however, disturbed by their inability to adjust budget priorities and Congress's lack of capacity to coordinate spending and taxing policy in concert with the economy. Congress's lack of control over the budget thus left it open to attacks from the Republicans in Congress and the president. If the budget were adopted all in a single piece, the reason for deficits would be more apparent and their defense would be made easier. Republicans could not propose overall spending reductions without also stating how those reductions might be achieved. Again, Roberts adheres to a procedural interpretation: "The liberal Democrats, of course, had an entirely different view of the Budget Act. They believed it would justify deficits as a necessary way to add enough spending

17. Paul Craig Roberts, *The Supply-Side Revolution* (Cambridge, Mass.: Harvard University Press, 1984), pp. 8–9.

to the economy to keep employment high, thereby defusing deficits as an issue. They were attracted to the prospect of having deficits sanctioned as a requirement of full-employment policy."[18]

In floor debate, this liberal interpretation of the act was articulated by Representatives Badillo and Matsunaga:

MR BADILLO: Mr. Speaker, I rise in support of this legislation. . . . By restoring the Congress to its proper role in the budget process this measure will correct the serious imbalance of power which for many years has rendered the legislative branch ineffective when faced with a better organized and more purposive Executive. . . . The Congress has been in a difficult position to achieve a meaningful reordering of national priorities because of our unwillingness to take the initiative to rationally manage the budget.

MR. MATSUNAGA: Mr. Speaker, if Congress is to resume its rightful place as a shaper of the policy of the United States, it must come to grips with the problems represented by the current fragmented process by which it considers the Federal Budget. I believe that the enactment of H.R. 7130 would be a necessary, even historic step toward that important goal.

18. Ibid.

These Democrats supported the act without giving the slightest hint that they expected it to reduce spending, yet many other members, Republicans generally, claimed to support the act precisely because they expected it to help reduce spending and deficits.

MR. TAYLOR: We all know that deficit spending has been one of the causes of inflation and many of our national problems. It is imperative that Congress face up to the responsibility of fiscal integrity, and this legislation should become a useful tool in securing this result.

MR. BAUMAN: In short, the Budget and Impoundment Control Act will give us the tools we need. . . . If we employ them intelligently, and combine them with a willingness to hold down the overall level of spending, then we may succeed in bringing fiscal responsibility to the Federal government for the first time in my memory.

MR. MARTIN: This bill would be helpful in the fight against inflation, because it provides hope for bringing Federal spending under control.[19]

Despite agreement on the precise form of the changes, Democrats and Republicans explained their support for the act quite differently. Any discussion of the act's purposes must take account of its diverse and conflicting defenses. It was not simply to reduce spending or to halt impoundments; in some sense it was, paradoxically, to do both. To understand the act we must be able to ex-

19. All these statements are from *Legislative History*, pp. 320, 349, 295, 319–320.

plain how the same piece of legislation could be seen to serve such contradictory ends. The answer, I think, is that neither conservatives nor liberals expected their goals to be achieved directly, but only by making the budget a matter of conscious deliberation and choice. Opponents of higher spending could convince themselves that spending increases would be harder to pass if considered in the context of their impact on the overall budget and the deficit. Supporters of those program increases could believe that conservative attacks on the level of spending and the deficit would be curtailed if one could propose spending reductions only by specifying where they would occur. Each side could convince itself that its purposes would best be served by the new process.

Ambiguity surrounds the act at least partly because of the very nature of procedural change, which does not produce policy change directly. Rather, procedures mediate between preference and actual choice. A procedural change alters the manner in which political pressures and individual preferences are brought to bear upon a choice, and only thus, indirectly, does a procedural change alter actual policy. Indirectness carries with it uncertainty. What would happen when members of Congress were required to vote on the aggregate budget and the deficit? One plausible hypothesis was that they would vote for smaller budgets and reduced deficits rather than risk defending large deficits before their constituents. But other scenarios were equally plausible. Possibly members of Congress, when faced with a choice between cutting spending and balancing the budget, would prefer not to cut spending. Or, forced to make choices, they might choose to reduce spending by cutting the military budget. Or they might raise taxes.

Or they might also do absolutely nothing. But no one could tell with any certainty how individuals would respond to the budget process, and so, absent any relevant experience or solid evidence, a single set of procedures was evidently seen to serve opposing purposes.

Whether the process has in fact had any identifiable impact on spending policy, it most certainly has significantly altered the distribution of power and influence in Congress. The budget process does create a legislative system in which majorities can adopt and enforce any budget policy they prefer, provided only that a majority can agree on a policy and agree to enforce it. This is an unprecedented situation in Congress, because at virtually all other times minorities within Congress—that is, mostly committees—have been able to block the expression of majority preference.

Skepticism about the Budget Process

In House floor debate on the Budget Act, Representative H. R. Gross, who was retiring at the end of the term, expressed a conventional skepticism about the behavior of Congress. "I will not be here when the alleged reform goes into operation," he explained, "but I predict Members of this House and members of the other body will quickly find ways to warp and bend the rules laid down today. . . . Mr. Speaker, this is another resort to gimmickry. This is again misleading the people."[20] Was the enactment of the Budget Act nothing more than a kind of hollow position-taking against the deficit, or was it a real effort to alter policy outcomes? A cynical observer of Congress could easily agree with Mr. Gross that rather

20. Ibid., p. 41.

than actually doing something about the deficit, which requires voting to cut programs, Congress indicated its symbolic opposition to deficits by voting for the process. Passing the Budget Act would take the heat off Congress temporarily, but it would do nothing about the deficit. In future years, this hypothesis suggests, Congress would use the adoption of a budget resolution as an occasion to vote for a tight budget with a small deficit. They would use the meaningless vote on the resolution to establish themselves as fiscal conservatives. Then they also would vote for generous spending increases that would contradict and supercede the resolution and claim credit with constituents for the benefits of that spending. The budget process could conceivably be twisted to serve the political purposes of Congress without having any effect on policy.

Evidence on this issue is mixed. Frequently, and inevitably, members of Congress have sought—successfully—to evade the strictures of the process they set up to discipline themselves. Committees have discovered ways of frustrating the purposes of the act, just as Gross predicted. This should only be expected, given what we know of the powerful forces toward decentralization in Congress. The trend over time, however, has been toward not a weaker process, but a stronger one. Conniving, duplicitous behavior has appeared, and Congress has acted to thwart it, thus preserving and increasing the integrity of the process. Reconciliation was initiated to correct the greatest single flaw in the process, its exemption of entitlements. A technique known as "deferred enrollment" has been used in a not entirely successful effort to keep the Appropriations Committee from playing games with its subcommittee allocation. Insistent complaints from the committees about how the process causes them great trouble also indicate that it disrupts and displeases committees, which is what one should expect from a real and meaningful budget process. Frequent waivers of Budget Act provisions were stripped by Gramm-Rudman. By moving toward greater coverage and stronger enforcement, Congress has confounded the predictions of Gross and other skeptics.

Evaluating the Budget Process

Observers are continually tempted to measure the success of the budget process by means of substantive criteria such as spending growth or deficit reduction. In view of the Budget Act supporters' inability to agree on the act's intended accomplishments, neither spending restraint nor any other substantive result constitutes a reasonable measure of success for the process. Spending results are, as Allen Schick claims, "a spurious test of budget control."[21] Both sides agreed on the desirability of integrating decisions about the whole of the budget and the parts. Success for the process must consist, then, not in any particular spending results, but in linking choices on the size of the budget and the deficit with choices on the parts. That is, neither deficits nor massive spending increases are problems, provided only that Congress authorizes them by a vote in the budget resolution and goes on the public record in favor. Likewise, if Congress votes in the resolution for spending reductions, then they must be made for the process to be regarded as successful. The crucial question is really whether the budget resolution corresponds at all closely to the actual budget. Advocates of spending reduction

21. Allen Schick, *Congress and Money* (Washington, D.C.: Urban Institute, 1980), p. 357.

Figure 5. Predicted and Actual Budget Deficits, FY 1976–1986

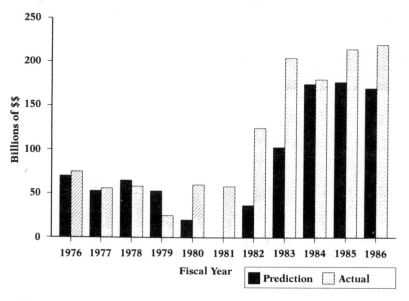

will not find this standard either appealing or compelling, but it is consistent with both the idea of a democratic legislature and the history of the act.

To what extent has Congress hidden behind the budget process? Has it used the process to avoid difficult votes? A number of measures could be devised to assess these matters; here I offer a simple, straightforward comparison of the deficit predicted in the resolution with the actual deficit. Deficits are politically charged, and a vote in favor of a resolution with a large deficit could be used by an electoral opponent against an incumbent. If Congress refuses to vote for deficits but also refuses to vote to restrain spending, we should expect large disparities between predicted and actual deficits. If predicted deficits are close to the actual, however, it suggests that the process is not fraudulent.

Figure 5 compares the size of the budget deficit predicted in the budget resolution with the actual budget deficit for the first decade of the budget process. Except for four years, from FY 1980 to 1983, budget deficits were relatively close to the deficit projected in the resolution. In both FY 1978 and 1979 the actual deficit was smaller than the projection, strongly indicating that in the early years of the process no systematic manipulation of figures was at work. From FY 1980 to 1983, budget deficits were wildly incorrect, systematically understating the size of the deficit; in at least the last three of these years resolutions were based on patently false estimates of revenue and expenditure that were used to produce an acceptably low deficit on paper. Subsequently, a relative degree of accuracy returned. From FY 1984 to 1988, budget resolutions frequently understated the true size of the deficit, but not to such a degree that the integrity of the resolution was vitiated.

For various reasons budget resolutions might not match actual performance: resolutions are based upon certain assumptions about economic performance, and if these assumptions should prove incorrect, revenues and expenditures will both be wrong. If the condition of the economy worsens, then revenues will be lessened, expenditures increased, and the deficit larger than projected. A better than anticipated economy produces higher revenues, lower expenditures, and a smaller deficit. Each year the budget committees invite a distinguished panel of economists to testify and offer their prognostications of economic performance, yet fluctuations in the economy nonetheless remain impossible to predict with any certainty. Thus it would be unreasonable to castigate Congress for inaccuracies in the budget resolution due to unforeseen changes in the economy.[22]

22. Rep. Les Aspin (D-Wis.) presented evidence indicating that from 1978 to 1980 economic change from forecasts was the greatest cause of spending diverging from resolutions. House Rules Commit-

Congress can also deliberately choose economic assumptions known to be incorrect, thus understating the
size of the budget deficit. This, of course, is precisely
what H. R. Gross would expect. Congress can and does
conjure up utterly false and misleading projections of
program spending levels and revenue levels to disguise
the real size of the deficit and avoid having to vote for
large deficits and high spending levels. Deceptive practices of this kind clearly subvert the budget process, and
if Congress consistently overestimates revenues while
underestimating expenditures and the deficit, something is seriously wrong in the process. The legislative
actions of Congress can also cause divergences from the
resolution. The adoption of new programs or increases
in existing programs, when the budget resolution did
not assume such changes, cause spending to rise above
the levels in the resolution. Similarly, if Congress fails to
adopt reductions assumed in the resolution, spending
targets will be violated.

All these problems have emerged, but inaccuracies in
the resolution due to unpredictable swings in the economy do not imply that Congress is attempting to circumvent the budget process. At issue are those dis-
crepancies resulting from deliberate manipulation of
economic projections and spending and revenue estimates. Although it is difficult to ascertain whether Congress knowingly adopted unrealistic estimates, we can
look for patterns. If estimates of spending and deficits
are consistently low and estimates of revenues consistently high, that constitutes prima facie evidence that
Congress is engaging in the duplicitous behavior Gross

---

tee, *Congressional Budget Process,* Hearings before the Task Force on
the Budget Process, 97th Cong., 2d sess. (USGPO, 1983), part 1, p. 35.

predicted. In fact, on all but two occasions the actual deficit has been larger than called for in the resolution; on all but four occasions actual spending has exceeded the figure in the resolution; and except for three instances, revenue estimates have exceeded actual revenues. Clearly, Congress has systematically erred in a direction that makes voting on the resolution easier, and few observers are likely to believe that this direction is an accident.

Although Congress has consistently underestimated deficits, in a number of cases the magnitude of the error has been relatively small. Members of Congress have apparently cheated, but the extent of their cheating has not usually been large enough to undermine the act's purposes. When, for example, the budget resolution for FY 1985 projected a deficit of $181 billion and the actual deficit was $31 billion higher, one could hardly argue that members of Congress were sleazily evading responsibility for their actions. They almost certainly fudged the figures to make it appear they were acting aggressively to reduce the deficit, but the fact remains that a majority of both chambers went on record backing—reluctantly—an absolutely huge deficit. Would their election prospects have been damaged had they been forced to vote for a deficit in excess of $200 billion? It is hard to imagine a public which accepts a $181 billion deficit rebelling because of a $212 billion deficit. A more serious problem was the FY 1981 budget resolution, in which Democrats concocted an imaginary budget surplus of $200 million to help them with the elections of 1980. Instead of a surplus there was a $58 billion deficit. The subsequent two years were no better, and possibly worse: projected deficits of $37 billion and $104 billion turned into actual deficits of $127.9 billion and $207.8

billion, respectively. In none of these years was there the slightest pretense of producing an accurate budget resolution. Political exigencies forced the authors of the resolutions to manipulate *assumptions* rather than *policy*—which is not how the budget process should work.

Assessing the accuracy of budget resolutions is one way of exploring the extent to which the budget process has produced a greater degree of budgetary control, but it is far from most useful. Unfortunately, measuring the accuracy of resolutions does little more than assess the accuracy of the assumptions upon which budget resolutions are based. It says nothing about either the extent to which the specific choices Congress makes over the course of a year are consistent with the resolution or whether Congress has the capacity to enforce the decisions reached in the resolution. A more important measure of the power and success of the budget process is the extent to which the budgetary choices that Congress makes subsequent to adopting a resolution are consistent with the resolution. If Congress can and does use the process to enforce budget cuts mandated by the resolution, or stops budget-busting legislation from passing, then one can conclude that Congress exercises deliberate control over the budget and that the budget process is used to constrain and alter behavior. In the following chapter I argue that developing the reconciliation process did provide such a capacity and that Congress has used the reconciliation process to enforce decisions. In the admittedly restricted sense of bestowing power over the budget upon congressional majorities, the process must be regarded a success.

3

Reconciliation and the Emergence of Majoritarian Politics

Much of the history of Congress has consisted of battles between majorities and minorities, with minorities—in the form of committees—typically succeeding in their efforts to retain the power to obstruct, delay, and otherwise prevent floor majorities from getting their way. Repeatedly in the history of Congress, committees, by refusing to produce legislation, have been able to frustrate floor majorities. On a number of occasions efforts have been made to subordinate committees to the preferences of the majority in the chamber, but these efforts have been only minimally effective. The best known means by which a majority in the House can overcome committee obstructionism is the discharge petition, first adopted in 1910 and modified several times in the next fifteen years. Despite great enthusiasm for a rule to discharge committees of jurisdiction over legislation, very few discharge petitions have succeeded. "Calendar Wednesday," adopted in 1909 as a way of getting bills to the floor over the objection of the

Rules Committee, proved so useless that Senator George Norris denounced it as "a homeopathic dose of nothingness."[1]

Through the budget process and reconciliation, Congress has become a majoritarian body, to a degree virtually unprecedented in modern times. Congressional majorities can adopt a comprehensive plan in a budget resolution and use reconciliation to press their decisions on committees—thus making the committees agents acting on the instructions of the whole. The normal sequence of the legislative process is profoundly altered. Normally committees act first by reporting legislation, and thus they determine the agenda of Congress. With reconciliation, the agenda for Congress, at least in the area of budgetary politics, is established by whatever group or entity is responsible for passing reconciliation instructions.

Committees still unquestionably dominate congressional organization, and they will continue in that role. Nonetheless, throughout the 1980s, the most important decisions made each year in Congress—about the nature of budget policy and the means of attaining it— have been made essentially outside the regular committee system, by the parties, caucuses, and bipartisan coalitions. When reconciliation first appeared, some observers doubted that it could long survive because it was so contrary to the normal organization of Congress.[2] But the organization of Congress is not immutable. It takes

1. Richard Lowitt, *George W. Norris: The Making of a Progressive, 1861–1912* (Syracuse: Syracuse University Press, 1963), p. 143.

2. In fall 1981, immediately after the massive Reagan budget victories, Allen Schick wrote: "Because Congress thrives on heterogeneity and fragmentation, it is this author's view that expanded reconciliation will not be a budget process for all legislative seasons." *PS* 14 (Fall 1981): 751.

the form it does for reasons that change, and when they do they can cause corresponding change in the structure of Congress. Huge deficits in the 1980s forced Congress to focus more on budgetary aggregates and less on the parts and thus encouraged members to search for organizational forms that provided a greater capacity to control the total.

This chapter documents the fact that use of the budget process since 1980 has shifted power out of committees and into majorities exerting their power on the floor. This argument involves showing that (1) budget resolutions have become important instruments for shaping policy, (2) control of the budget resolutions' content is very directly in the hands of congressional majorities, and (3) these majorities are assembled by means of negotiations conducted in extracommittee bodies.

How Reconciliation Works

The use of the term "reconciliation" is paradoxical; it implies the resolution of conflict, yet it has generated some of the most strenuous conflict in Congress in memory. The name, nonetheless, is appropriate because the purpose of reconciliation is to "reconcile" individual program spending levels with an overall budgetary ceiling.

Reconciliation's procedure is fairly simple in theory. In the spring, Congress adopts a budget resolution for the coming fiscal year, which begins October 1. The resolution establishes an overall spending ceiling as well as a distribution of that spending among functional allocations. When the allocation for a committee is below its current spending level, either spending on programs must be reduced, or the ceilings will be exceeded. "Reconciliation instructions" are directives to specific committees to reduce spending on programs in their jurisdictions by indicated amounts.[3] Typical reconciliation language might read: "The Senate [or House] Committee on Agriculture shall report changes in laws within the jurisdiction of that committee sufficient to reduce budget authority by $200,000,000 and outlays by $200,000,000 in fiscal year 1988."[4] Typically, between ten and fifteen committees will be instructed to make reductions, in amounts ranging from several million to more than a billion dollars. The tax committees—Ways and Means and Finance—have also been instructed to raise revenue.

These instructions are part of budget resolutions and must be passed in identical form by both chambers, just like ordinary legislation. Reconciliation instructions are clear and unmistakable signals to committees that the body as a whole wants them to make certain changes in their programs.

After passing a budget resolution that includes reconciliation instructions, committees are supposed to go

3. With one exception, reconciliation instructions have directed committees to reduce spending only in entitlement programs. Programs that receive authorizations and appropriations are thus not generally covered by reconciliation. In 1981 (FY 1982), authorizations as well as entitlements were reconciled. In retrospect, this was universally conceded to be a bad idea, and it has not been attempted again. By reconciling authorizations, the budget process intrudes too far into the jurisdiction of the appropriations committees, which are normally thought to be responsible for restraining spending in authorized programs. Reconciling authorizations leaves the appropriations committees with essentially nothing to do. However, for the appropriations committees to make very large reductions deprives authorizing committees of control over their programs.

4. In most cases, committees have been instructed to make reductions over a period of three years.

to work immediately, writing legislation that will satisfy their reconciliation targets. Committees are completely free to determine how to meet their targets; their instructions concern only the amount of savings they must produce. Budget resolutions are always based upon fairly specific assumptions about how the targets might be reached, although committees are not compelled to do as the budget committees suggest. In some cases—for instance, when a committee has only one entitlement program or only one program large enough to yield the required reductions—committees have virtually no discretion in making reconciliation cuts. Normally the resolution directs committees to complete their work by a certain midsummer date. They then send their legislation to their chamber's budget committee.

The budget committees perform a purely ministerial function in assembling the various committee reports into a single, often massive, reconciliation bill. They are forbidden by the Budget Act to make substantive changes of any kind in the committees' legislation. All the reconciliation legislation from all the instructed committees, packaged together, then proceeds to the floor of each chamber where it is debated, possibly amended, and voted upon.[5] When, as is invariably the case, House and Senate versions are not identical, a conference committee must be formed to resolve whatever differences exist. As is the case with all legislation, the president has the opportunity to sign or veto a reconciliation bill.

5. Evidently, reconciliation bills always pass when they reach the floor, and normally they pass overwhelmingly. They are equated so unambiguously with spending restraint that few members wish to oppose them, even when opposed to particular provisions.

The Need for Reconciliation

If members want Congress to enact narrow distributive legislation, providing dams, roads, post offices, and other items of direct electoral benefit to members, the committee system of Congress is perhaps uniquely well suited for their purposes.[6] The passage of pork-barrel legislation can occur through a decentralized committee system because little explicit coordination is required and enforcing bargains is not a problem. Norms of reciprocity and universalism—"you pass my pork-barrel bill, and I'll pass yours"—largely take care of the problem of coordination.[7] The informality of this mode of coordination is indicated by the following exchange on the Senate floor during the debate on the National Parks and Recreation Act of 1978, a bill known as the "Park Barrel" bill because it provided for so many new projects in so many states.

> "Is there any state other than Kansas that did not end up with a park?" asked Sen. Robert Dole, R-Kan.
> "Did we leave you out, Bob?" asked Sen. James Abourezk, D-S.D., chairman of the Energy Subcommittee on parks and the floor manager of the bill.

6. By "direct" benefits, I mean those provided to identifiable persons, benefitting specific constituencies—and also specific members of Congress. "Indirect" benefits are received, not in the form of a monthly check, but through a reduced deficit, for instance. Reducing direct benefits to individual A may provide an indirect benefit to individual B.

7. Donald Matthews, "Folkways of the United States Senate," *American Political Science Review* 53 (Dec. 1959): 1064–1089. Barry Weingast, "A Rational Choice Perspective on Congressional Norms," *American Journal of Political Science* 23 (May 1979): 245–261. Kenneth Shepsle and Barry Weingast, "Political Preference for the Pork Barrel: A Generalization," *American Journal of Political Science* 25 (Feb. 1981): 96–111.

"I have two more years in my term," noted Dole, as laughter continued in the chamber. Sen. Clifford P. Hansen, R-Wyo., also on the subcommittee, offered Dole a little sympathy. "It is my understanding that six states—five others—did not make it." "I appreciate that," replied Dole. "We will have a meeting later."[8]

This brief colloquy illustrates a form of coordination without central control, wherein Dole serves notice that he expects his turn will come, within two years.

The need for coordination in distributive politics is diminished by the convenient fit of narrow policies within the jurisdictions of single committees, obviating the need for intercommittee negotiations. Enforcing implicit bargains is not a source of difficulty; it is not normally a problem to get the Interior Committee to approve new parks or the Public Works Committee to recommend new public works. If anything, it is disproportionately to the benefit of members of these and other committees to report such legislation. The problem has more often been holding them back than stirring them to action.

Broader policies—such as reducing deficits, restraining spending, and enacting consistent fiscal policy—are not well served by a committee system.[9] In large measure these goals can be attained only by altering or curtailing existing distributive policies. Doing so involves a

8. *CQ Almanac, 1978*, pp. 704–705.
9. "The rules of germaneness and of jurisdiction make intercommittee agreements difficult to arrange except in special circumstances. The informal practices of both chambers still discourage members from involving themselves in legislation considered in other committees." John Ferejohn, "Congress and Redistribution," in *Making Economic Policy in Congress*, ed. Allen Schick (Washington, D.C.: American Enterprise Institute, 1983), p. 135.

direct cost, and only indirect benefits, to constituents. Such policies span numerous or even perhaps all committee jurisdictions. Under these circumstances, the easy informality that allowed Dole to joke about the absence of a park for Kansas—and to assume that he would get one before the next election—must be replaced by more explicit, formal coordination. Broad legislation that overlaps several committees' jurisdictions or policies whose success depends on simultaneous, coordinated actions by multiple committees do not move well through the fragmented structures of Congress. Logically, logrolling can occur in a downward direction; it is entirely conceivable that the indirect benefits of cutting a series of programs will exceed the direct costs. But legislation enacting such an exchange will be able to pass only under special circumstances.

The problem of spending restraint in Congress can be understood as a problem of collective action. When one member must endure the sacrifice of a program dear to his or her district so that all members may benefit from deficit control, he will demand that other members make similar sacrifices. One committee will be reluctant to cut programs in its jurisdiction without an assurance that other committees are doing likewise. Senator Bob Packwood (R-Ore.), chairman of the Senate Finance Committee, explicitly raised this issue in 1985. "The Finance Committee," he wrote, "will meet its responsibility for achieving $51.2 billion in savings . . . *IF ALL OTHER MAJOR COMMITTEES CAN MEET THE SPENDING CUTS TOTALS REQUIRED OF THEM.*"[10]

10. Senate Budget Committee, *First Concurrent Resolution on the Budget FY 1986*, S. Rept. 99–15, 99th Cong., 1st sess. (USGPO, 1985), p. 165; emphasis in the original. The savings Packwood refers to are those recommended by the Office of Management and Budget.

Even when spending restraint is desired by members of Congress and when they are willing to exchange direct benefits to their districts in order to cut the deficit, legislators will not necessarily be able to enact deficit reduction measures. Deficit reduction legislation will normally succeed only when there is a structure to facilitate intercommittee bargaining and when the agreements so reached can be enforced. Success at cutting the budget has come in the past several years because the reconciliation procedure overcomes these defects of normal congressional organization. It is inconceivable that Dole, or Packwood, or any committee chair, would say, "Okay. I'll cut my programs this year because I know you will cut yours next year." That degree of trust does not exist in Congress. An informally coordinated reciprocity works well only when it distributes benefits, not costs.

The Budget Process without Reconciliation

Shortly after becoming the first staff director of the House Budget Committee (HBC), Walter Kravitz explained that his goal was "to make the passage of budget resolutions just as routine as the passage of appropriations bills."[11] To some extent, the budget committees behaved like ordinary committees and passed their resolutions in a relatively routine fashion. The budget committees held hearings, received testimony from expert witnesses, wrote budget resolutions in protracted committee markup sessions, and generally acted like

11. Quoted in John Ellwood, "Comments," in *Federal Budget Policy in the 1980s*, ed. Gregory Mills and John Palmer (Washington, D.C.: Urban Institute, 1984), p. 378. Ellwood believes that the reconciliation process has become routinized through the use of reconciliation three years running. But the manner of its use, always different, has been anything but routine.

normal committees. When budget resolutions went to the floor, they usually passed with few amendments.

The apparent success of the budget committees disguised a fundamental weakness. Passage of budget resolutions will be routine only when they are unimportant and do not change policy. A budget resolution that matters—for instance, shifting budgetary priorities, cutting spending, or raising revenues—will be immensely important; it becomes the object of such intense controversy that no single committee can or should retain control over it. For the budget committees to exercise the same kind of control over budget resolutions as the House Appropriations Committee does over its bills would entail the concentration of vast amounts of power in one committee, making the budget committees more like a cabinet than a committee. Because members of Congress who do not sit on the budget committees would never willingly consent to relinquish such power, it is not reasonable to expect that budget resolutions written by and controlled by the budget committees will have significant influence over budget policy.

In the mid- to late 1970s, budget resolutions passed on the floor of the House and the Senate almost exactly as drafted by the budget committees. We should not conclude on that evidence alone that the committees exercised influence over budget policy. According to Allen Schick's definitive study of the budget process in its first years, the process was used not to reduce spending but rather to bestow congressional approval on a level of spending that would have occurred regardless of the process. Schick reports: "In almost a hundred interviews with members of Congress and staffers, no one expressed the view that the allocations in the budget resolutions had knowingly been set below legislative expectations. 'We got all that we needed,' one committee staff director exulted."[12] The budget committees largely "accommodated" themselves to the desire of the other committees, and accordingly they were able to pass their budget resolutions without many floor amendments. When resolutions came to be meaningful statements of policy, control over them passed to other bodies.

Edmund Muskie (D-Maine) and Henry Bellmon (R-Okla.), the first chairman and ranking member of the Senate Budget Committee, set out at the inauguration of the new process in 1975 to create a bipartisan Senate committee. Both were committed to the success of the process, and to that end they established an excellent working relationship that permitted the committee to function on a bipartisan basis. Over the first five years of the committee's life, there was an extraordinary degree of minority party participation in writing resolutions. Sometimes more than half of all successful motions in committee markup of first budget resolutions were sponsored by the minority Republicans, and never before 1980 (FY 1981) did minority motions account for fewer than a third of all successful motions. In a partisan committee the minority would be excluded from meaningful participation.

The Senate Budget Committee (SBC) met at great length to produce their resolutions. First the full committee would debate and vote upon each of the nineteen functions in the budget, one by one, to find a level of spending for each that would command the support of a majority of the committee. When this process was complete they would work through a second time for the

12. Allen Schick, *Congress and Money* (Washington, D.C.: Urban Institute, 1980), p. 313.

purpose of lowering the spending total. This function-by-function analysis and its reiteration absorbed much time and filled many pages of transcript. The vast length of these committee markup sessions indicates strongly that the committee did not merely ratify a resolution produced by the chair or the majority party caucus but wrote resolutions in the course of markup.

SBC resolutions passed on the floor by substantial margins and with few amendments. Muskie equated floor involvement in the writing of resolutions with the demise of the process, and in this period floor amendments did not often pass. On the floor, Muskie, a liberal, argued against amendments that sought to increase spending, while Bellmon, a conservative, led the fight against cuts.[13] Their view was that the budget process was "incapable of surviving the rough and tumble of floor action"; for this reason the committee resolution must prevail.[14] Majority Leader Mike Mansfield supported this deference to the committee, saying, "I intend to support fully what the Budget Committee has recommended because if we do not then I think we might as well abolish it, and go back to our old ways."[15] Budget control seemed to hinge on the success of the budget committees.

In the view of leading senators, the budget committees were not to lead but to follow the wishes of Congress. They were to accept and respond to the initiatives of other committees, not constrain them. Muskie explained his view that the function of the SBC was "to reflect a consensus of the Senate on issues insofar as evi-

13. Ibid., pp. 282–283.
14. Ibid., p. 283.
15. Ibid., pp. 284–285; *Cong. Rec.*, May 4, 1977, p. S7048.

dence of a consensus is available to us."[16] Robert Dole expressed a similarly modest view of the SBC: "The Budget Committees should not pass spending targets that force the adoption of program changes that have not even been contemplated. It has been and should continue to be the Budget Committee's practice to reflect in its spending targets and score-keeping the budget effects of pending legislation that appears to have some possibility of passing."[17] Early floor success of the budget committees bespeaks neither the power of the committees nor of the process, but an acceptance of an inferior position. Accommodation does not make a committee powerful.

Assumed Legislative Savings

Yet from 1976 to 1979 the budget committees did attempt to depart somewhat from the pattern of accommodation by means of the "assumed legislative savings" approach to entitlement control. The budget process as originally enacted did include various means to prevent appropriations from exceeding the targets in the resolutions. However, a compromise in the writing of the Budget Act essentially exempted entitlement programs from the controls of the process. Nonetheless, the budget committees wrote resolutions based upon assumptions that certain committees would report legislation reducing spending on their entitlements. If the committees did not produce these savings, spending would exceed the targets in the resolution.

Assumed legislative savings was nothing more than

16. Schick, *Congress and Money*, p. 311.
17. Ibid., pp. 311–312.

an unenforceable request by the budget committees that other committees change their programs. Few informed observers should have been surprised that the committees were not forthcoming; indeed, these committees were derelict in their responsibilities and produced only trivial proportions of the assumed savings. The failure of the assumed legislative savings approach ultimately caused the budget committees to seek more effective tools.

In July 1979, Muskie became concerned about the lack of committee compliance with the legislative savings and sent letters to the leaders and ranking members of the appropriate committees, requesting that they take action. Muskie warned each of them that unless they reported the requested changes, the deficit would grow. Blandly the leaders replied that while they agreed that the deficit was a problem, they did not believe cutting *their* programs was the best solution. Respectfully they declined to obey the injunctions of the budget resolutions.[18] The ease with which the substantive committees eluded budget committee attempts to broaden the budgetary net undoubtedly contributed to the floor success of resolutions. Knowing that they would later be able to ignore the resolution, committees had made no efforts on the floor to strip the resolution of proposed savings.[19] The SBC took umbrage at this sort of behavior: "The First Budget resolution assumed re-

18. The correspondence between Muskie and the other chairmen is included as an appendix in Senate Budget Committee, *Second Concurrent Resolution on the Budget, FY 1980*, S. Rept. 96–311, 96th Cong., 1st sess. (USGPO, 1979), pp. 195–248.

19. As Schick explains, "These committees therefore opt for silence when the budget resolution is debated in the expectation that their inaction will force the Budget Committees to restore the funds later in the year." *Congress and Money*, pp. 318–319.

ductions in outlays of $5.6 billion. No voice was raised against that policy on the Senate floor. Indeed, many a speech has endorsed the policy of frugality. Many a press release has broadcast a firm commitment to the painful politics of austerity. But as this report is filed, it is clear that the rhetoric has not been reflected in policy."[20]

Initiating Reconciliation

In 1980, matters changed decisively. Reconciliation replaced legislative savings, and the focus of spending reduction efforts shifted out of the budget committees, ultimately to the floor.

The SBC had moved tentatively to initiate the use of reconciliation in 1979, after the committee chairs refused to comply with their assigned legislative savings. Frustrated by the nonchalance with which committees had been able to ignore the first resolution, the SBC included the legislative savings in the second resolution, in the form of reconciliation instructions to the committees. This first attempt to invoke the procedure was a committee initiative, intended to provide for enhanced enforcement of the committee's own resolution. There was some dissent on the Senate floor, but a motion to delete the reconciliation language failed. The Senate's second concurrent resolution on the budget for FY 1980 thus called for reconciliation; the House resolution, however, did not.

In conference the House side argued successfully that the timing of the budget process did not favor use of reconciliation to achieve substantial legislative changes.

20. Senate Budget Committee, *Second Concurrent Resolution on the Budget, FY 1980,* S. Rept. 96–311, 96th Cong., 1st sess. (USGPO, 1979), pp. 6–7.

The second resolution should be passed by September 15, and the reconciliation bill, implementing legislative changes mandated by the resolution, is to be passed ten days later. On October 1, the fiscal year begins. Attempting to speed up the legislative process to that extent is infeasible, especially if nontrivial changes are required. Moreover, the official schedule of the reconciliation process is incompatible with the Constitution. The Constitution allows the president ten days to veto legislation, whereas the budget process provides only a week between passage of the reconciliation bill and the start of the fiscal year. Perceiving the seriousness of these difficulties, the Senate conferees receded from their position, and the reconciliation language was dropped. But the possibility of using reconciliation to reduce entitlements was not forgotten.

Shortly after President Carter submitted his FY 1981 budget proposal to Congress on January 28, 1980, inflation and interest rates soared. A weak economy, high inflation, and rising interest rates augured badly for Democratic electoral fortunes in the fall elections. Acting on the belief that the $15.8 billion deficit in Carter's budget had adversely affected the bond markets, Democrats from House and Senate leadership and both budget committees met with representatives from the White House in order to produce a new and, they hoped, balanced budget. In a series of meetings lasting some ten days the participants put together a package of spending cuts and tax increases designed to produce a "balanced" budget, achieved only by using unrealistically optimistic economic projections. But the unlikelihood that the package would produce budgetary balance was not as important as the agreement that some entitlement programs should be cut.

Having reached agreement on a package of legislative changes, the problem of getting them enacted remained. Experience over the previous years with legislative savings made clear that this was not trivial. To overcome some problems inherent in cutting the budget, they decided to depart from strict adherence to the Budget Act and employ the reconciliation procedure on the first resolution. According to the letter of the Budget Act, reconciliation is a device to enforce the ceilings in the second. But because the Budget Act stipulates that the first resolution may contain "such other matters relating to the budget as may be appropriate to carry out the purposes of this Act," it was deemed legally and procedurally acceptable to shift reconciliation from late in the process to early. In due course, parliamentary rulings affirmed the legitimacy of this informal but important modification of the budget process.

Introducing reconciliation profoundly altered the authorship of resolutions. Prior to 1980 budget resolutions, written in the budget committees, were the result of long negotiations conducted among the committee members. The manner of the negotiations conducted by each committee was quite different; the HBC was highly partisan, and the SBC bipartisan. Nonetheless, decisions were made in the committees, and these decisions, though far from earth-shattering, subsequently were accepted by floor majorities. The pattern of budget resolutions being written in budget committees was altered in 1980 when the committees instead performed a largely ministerial function. Instead of negotiating the resolution within themselves, the committees took the budget as rewritten by the leadership group and drafted it into the form of a budget resolution. The budget committees made some changes but generally adhered to the agreements worked out previously by the leadership. Both committee-reported resolutions included reconciliation instructions.

Reconciliation on the first resolution constitutes a repudiation of the original agreements of 1974 that exempted existing entitlements from budget process control. The significance of these developments was not lost on the defenders of committee prerogatives. The day after the HBC reported its resolution, most House committee chairs sent a letter of protest to Speaker O'Neill:

> We are opposed to the inclusion of reconciliation in the First Concurrent Resolution on the Budget. . . . Given the time available to the Budget Committee, it is impossible for it to become well enough acquainted with all federal programs and activities to know where to apply appropriate economies program by program. The standing committees, with expertise in the programs in their respective jurisdictions, should attempt to translate the targets into program detail. Invoking reconciliation in the first step of the congressional budget process undermines the committee system, reposing in the Budget Committee authority to legislate substantively with respect to the nature and scope of federal activities.[21]

One may take the leaders' protest as either a principled defense of committees or a reflex response to an invasion of their traditional rights. But however impeccable the chairs' logic, it seems somehow the case that when committees "attempt to translate the targets into program detail," somehow the targets are invari-

21. This letter is reproduced in House Budget Committee, *A Review of the Reconciliation Process,* Committee Print, 98th Cong., 2nd sess. (USGPO, 1984), p. 19.

ably missed. The structure the chairs defend is simply inappropriate to the task of budget cutting. So when the political circumstances for whatever reason demand that budgets be cut, committees will of necessity be, to some extent, supplanted by other structures and procedures more conducive to that goal. When the HBC resolution came to the floor in the House, a Morris Udall (D-Ariz.) motion to strip the resolution of reconciliation language failed, 127–289.[22]

Upon passage of the resolution, committees had until June 15 to report their reconciliation legislation. Grudgingly, they more or less complied with their reconciliation directives.[23] On June 30, facing little opposition, the reconciliation bill passed in the Senate, and on September 4 the House passed its reconciliation bill. After an arduous conference committee, the conference report was passed by both houses, and the first reconciliation bill in history was signed into law by President Carter. Thus, under Democratic party auspices, a full and complete system of congressional budget control was established.

Reconciliation is commonly believed to have been initiated in 1981 by David Stockman, when the process was used to serve Republican purposes. Had the Democrats not inaugurated reconciliation by shifting it to the first resolution, it would not have been available for

22. *CQ Weekly Report,* May 10, 1980, pp. 1228–1229.
23. There was, however, plenty of cheating by the committees. One particularly transparent trick was to delay an intergovernmental payment from September until October. This did not reduce total spending at all, only spending in FY 1981. Efforts of this kind led to the adoption of multiyear reconciliation in successive reconciliation instructions. By requiring committees to cut spending over three years, they are deprived of the opportunity simply to shift spending to the next year. However, they can still shift spending to a *previous* fiscal year, for the same devious purpose.

Stockman in 1981. It is doubtful that the House parliamentarian, an appointee of the Speaker, would have allowed reconciliation on the first resolution, to the benefit of Ronald Reagan's program, had the precedent not been set the previous year.

Enhanced Importance of Budget Resolutions

From 1980 to 1987, Congress passed a reconciliation bill every year, confounding the expectations of observers who viewed reconciliation as too contrary to the ordinary fragmented and decentralized tendencies of Congress to survive. Examining the record of Congress in enacting reconciliation bills, one could argue that the process has been a failure. Committees regularly cheat in producing savings, claiming credit for more savings than actually appear. Reconciliation bills have often been enacted late; consequently the savings realized are reduced. Reconciliation bills have also increased expenditures by including large amounts of extraneous matter inserted by committees because they know a reconciliation bill is sure to pass. Such behavior is exactly what one would expect from committees, whose members tend to support the programs in their jurisdictions and prefer not to cut them.

There are also impediments other than committee obstruction to the final enactment of reconciliation legislation, and these have often been more troublesome. In 1983, for example, both the House and the Senate passed their reconciliation bills, but disagreements between the House, the Senate, and the president delayed final enactment of the legislation until April 5, 1984—some five months after the budget committees reported the original reconciliation bills. One can hardly blame the budget process or the reconciliation procedure for failing to overcome the inefficiencies stemming from separation of powers.[24]

Congress and its committees have not implemented reconciliation perfectly, but the failure to attain perfection should not cause us to dismiss the process. To an impressive extent, congressional committees have responded to their reconciliation instructions and have complied with the demands of their chambers. Legislation cutting spending and raising taxes—legislation not enacted under ordinary legislative procedure—has been enacted with the help of reconciliation. The extent of committee compliance with reconciliation is particularly impressive when compared with that under "assumed legislative savings." Without an effective enforcement mechanism, committees routinely ignored the urgings of the budget committees to reduce expenditures, and only minute proportions of the assumed savings were actually enacted. Under reconciliation, far larger proportions of the savings targeted in the resolution have been enacted. Table 1 compares assumed legislative savings and reconciliation and shows that compliance with the resolution has improved markedly since the introduction of reconciliation. This table strongly suggests that, since 1980, budget resolutions have been meaningful statements of policy, whereas previously they were ignored.

Insofar as floor majorities have been able to agree on spending reductions, committees have not impeded their enactment. With reconciliation, budget resolutions are transformed from more or less symbolic documents to effective means of enforcing majority pref-

24. See *CQ Almanac, 1984,* p. 160.

Table 1

Comparison of Legislative Savings and Reconciliation:
Success in Achieving Spending Reductions
(amounts in millions of dollars)

Year	Savings Recommended in Resolution	Savings Adopted in Legislation	Percentage Adopted
Assumed Legislative Savings			
1976 (FY 1977)	$3,027	$200	6.6
1977 (FY 1978)	$1,944	$0	0.0
1978 (FY 1979)	$2,251	$19	0.8
1979 (FY 1980)	$6,000	?	?
Reconciliation			
1980 (FY 1981)	$6,400	$4,631	72.3
1981 (FY 1982)	$35,116	$35,190	100.0
1982 (FY 1983)	$27,116	$30,300	111.4
1983 (FY 1984)	$12,300	$10,300	83.7 (House)[a]
	$12,300	$14,600	119.7 (Senate)
1984 (FY 1985)	—	—	
1985 (FY 1986)	$75,500	$60,900	80.6 (House)[b]
	$75,500	$85,700	113.5 (Senate)
1986 (FY 1987)	$24,200	$15,200	62.8 (House)[c]
	$24,200	$12,600	52.1 (Senate)

SOURCES: House Budget Committee, *A Review of the Reconciliation Process*, Committee Print, 98th Cong., 2nd sess. (USGPO, November 1984), and *CQ Almanac* (Washington, D.C.: Congressional Quarterly Press, various years).

[a]House entries are for H.R. 4169, the House-passed reconciliation bill. It was not enacted into law until 1984 because of the Senate's failure to pass a corresponding bill. Senate entries are for S. 2032, the Senate reconciliation bill. Reported from the Senate Budget Committee, it was composed of legislation produced by authorizing committees. It never came to a floor vote in 1983 because of a conflict between the Budget and the Finance committees about amending the bill on the floor to include revenue increases.

[b]The 1985 entries are for H.R. 3500, the two House-passed reconciliation bills, and S. 1730, the Senate-passed reconciliation bill. The FY 1986 reconciliation bill, which should have passed prior to October 1, 1985, did not pass until March 20, 1986, because of a dispute between the House and the Senate over the Superfund. By that time half of FY 1986 had already elapsed, and the actual savings realized were diminished accordingly. OMB provided a radically different estimate of the savings, contending that even if the reconciliation bill had been enacted on time, the House bill would have yielded savings of $17.5 billion and the Senate bill only $22.2 billion. The savings reported here were, however, certified by the CBO. *CQ Almanac, 1985* (Washington, D.C.: Congressional Quarterly Press, 1986), pp. 507, 509.

[c]The entries for 1986 are for the bills passed by the House and Senate, H.R. 5300 and S. 2706. The final reconciliation bill, H.R. 5300, yielded savings of $11.7 billion; the reduction was due to compromises in the conference committee. *CQ Almanac, 1986* (Washington, D.C.: Congressional Quarterly Press, 1987), pp. 559, 574.

erence. As the budget resolution has become more important, the surrounding politics has become far more contentious, and power over the content has shifted away from the budget committees.

Budget Negotiations after 1980

No consistent pattern in the authorship of budget resolutions has emerged since 1980, except that budget committees have generally not been the forum in which the policy embodied in the resolution has been negotiated. With impressive regularity, either the committees have adopted as their own budgets developed elsewhere, or the resolutions they report have been defeated or fundamentally altered on the floor. The budget committees have ceased to function as independent, autonomous decision-making bodies. Table 2 shows briefly the origins of the first budget resolutions that have passed each chamber, beginning in 1980 (FY 1981). Given the dominance of the budget committees over budget resolutions prior to 1980, the shift of budget influence since then represents a remarkable change.

An examination of adopting budget resolutions in the past several years shows that neither budget committees nor any other organized entity within Congress (or outside) is able to exercise consistent control over the process. Over the period 1980–1984, there were five complete budget cycles, each of which followed a markedly different pattern. Sometimes the majority party prevailed, but frequently it did not. Occasionally an ad hoc bipartisan coalition passed the resolution, but frequently the votes came almost solely from one party. Upon occasion the president occupied a prominent position in the proceedings, but often he did not. The bud-

Table 2
Sources of Budget Resolutions, 1980–1987

Senate	House

1980 (FY 1981)

Leadership meeting drafts resolution, and those agreements are largely accepted in the SBC. SBC resolution passes on the floor.	The same leadership agreements are accepted by the HBC. HBC resolution passes on the floor.

1981 (FY 1982)

SBC reports resolution that mirrors Reagan's recommendation. It passes on the floor.	HBC Democrats report a resolution incorporating some but not all of Reagan's budget proposals, but it is defeated on the floor by the Gramm-Latta I substitute.

1982 (FY 1983)

SBC Republicans draft and report a resolution, but it is reworked in the Republican caucus before being passed on the floor.	HBC Democrats report a resolution, which is defeated on the floor by a Republican substitute.

1983 (FY 1984)

SBC cannot agree to a resolution and consequently reports a perfunctory version merely to allow the process to continue. Bipartisan substitute passes on the floor.	Jones-O'Neill budget plan wins in the HBC and passes on the floor.

1984 (FY 1985)

SBC adopts a resolution that reflects the "Rose Garden" agreement between Senate Republican leaders and the president.	HBC reports two resolutions, one favored by the leadership and the other by junior members of the committee. The latter, known as "pay-as-you-go," passes on the floor.

Table 2
(*continued*)

Senate	House
1985 (FY 1986)	
SBC reports a "turkey" to keep the process going. Dole, the majority leader, negotiates a compromise budget with the president, and this passes on the floor.	HBC Democrats poll their party with "An Exercise in Hard Choices" and devise a resolution with the help of the party caucus. Committee resolution passes on the floor.
1986 (FY 1987)	
SBC revolts against Reagan's budget and produces a bipartisan resolution. Dole reaches compromise with the White House and passes partial substitute on the floor.	HBC Democrats produce compromise between liberals and conservatives. HBC resolution passes on the floor with strong party support.

get committees will not disappear given their vital role in enforcing resolutions, but there is no basis upon which the budget committees will be able to exercise substantial control over meaningful budget resolutions. Rather, as long as budget policy is conducted through budget resolutions and reconciliation, we should expect instability to continue as the norm.[25]

1981

The election of Ronald Reagan as president was almost universally interpreted as a repudiation of Democratic policies, and it caused many Democrats to be more than normally inclined to cut the budget. On February 18, newly installed President Reagan detailed a new budget calling for large spending and tax cuts in his first speech

25. See John Ellwood, "Comments," p. 378.

to the Congress. It was not Reagan's intention to wait until the second year of his presidency to see his budget priorities enacted—a fate often forced on new presidents by the inconvenient schedule of the budget cycle. Three weeks after the congressional address, OMB released a detailed, program-by-program documentation of Reagan's revision of Carter's last budget.[26]

As in 1980, there arose the question of how to get Congress to enact a complex policy that reached into the jurisdictions of many committees and was likely to be opposed by those committees. Again, reconciliation was chosen as the best means.

Several weeks before the normal date to begin work on the first budget resolution, the SBC, controlled by Republicans, began the budget process by reporting out reconciliation instructions. Because of Democratic fears of a turn to the right in the electorate, they largely went along with the Republican majority as the committee drafted reconciliation instructions that mirrored the president's recommended budget. The committee exercised little or no independence. Indeed, even small departures from the president's budget were not allowed by some committee members. When, for example, the draft budget resolution suggested by Chairman Pete Domenici (R-N.M.) called for budget deficits of $60 billion in 1984, contrary to the president's official position that the budget would be balanced by then, three Republicans on the committee refused to support Domenici. He was forced to add future unspecified savings under "allowances."[27] The reconciliation resolution, Senate Con-

26. Office of Management and Budget, *Fiscal Year 1982 Budget Revisions* (Washington, D.C.: OMB, March 1981).

27. See Senate Budget Committee, *First Concurrent Resolution on the Budget, Fiscal Year 1982*, S. Rept. 97–49, 97th Cong., 1st sess.

current Resolution 9, came to the floor unencumbered by the full trappings of a budget resolution. Reporting reconciliation instructions without a full budget resolution was unorthodox, but it was explained as necessary to give Senate committees extra time to produce their legislation. In the full Senate the resolution was met by Democratic opposition and resolute Republican support. Democrats offered numerous amendments, and all were turned aside by a highly unified Republican party. Somewhat later, the SBC reported a more orthodox, complete budget resolution. Another perfect reflection of presidential priorities, it met similar receptions in both committee and chamber. But on the vote for final passage, a majority of Democrats supported the resolution, and it passed by a wider margin than any previous budget resolution in the Senate, 78–20.

On the House side, James Jones (D-Okla.), the new chairman of the HBC, was faced with the challenge of producing and passing a Democratic resolution despite a diminished Democratic majority. His plan was to cooperate with the president, but only including about 75 percent of the president's recommended cuts in the resolution. By calling for smaller tax cuts and a smaller de-

---

(USGPO, 1981), pp. 196, 198. The unspecified savings were the "magic asterisk" referred to by David Stockman. According to William Greider, "somehow or other, the Senate Budget Committee staff insisted upon putting honest numbers in its resolution—the projected deficits of $60 billion plus running through 1984. That left the Republican senators staring directly at the same scary numbers that Stockman and the Wall Street analysts had already seen. . . . After a few days of reassurances, Stockman persuaded the Republican senators to relax about the future, and two weeks later they passed the resolution—without being given any concrete assurances as to where he would find future cuts of such magnitude. In effect, the 'magic asterisk' sufficed." William Greider, *The Education of David Stockman and Other Americans* (New York: Dutton, 1982), pp. 36–37.

fense spending increase, Jones's resolution managed to project a smaller deficit for FY 1982 than either the president's or the Senate's budget. In committee, Jones's resolution was adopted by a party-line vote.

Trouble awaited the HBC resolution on the floor. In every previous year the Republican minority had challenged the committee-reported resolution on the floor with a substitute resolution, but prior to 1981 they had never won. In 1981, Phil Gramm, a Texas Democrat newly appointed to the HBC, joined the minority in sponsoring a challenge to the House resolution.[28] Gramm, OMB Director David Stockman, and Minority Whip and House Budget Committee member Delbert Latta (R-Ohio) drafted an alternative resolution that incorporated all the president's budget and tax recommendations. The substitute resolution, known as Gramm-Latta, was widely favored to win,[29] and it did, by the surprisingly large margin of 253–176—with sixty-three Democrats and all Republicans voting for the amendment. The resolution required thirteen committees in the Senate and fifteen in the House to report legislation producing total first year cuts of about $35 billion. The committees named in the resolution were to send their legislation to their respective budget committees by June 15.

Unsurprisingly, the Senate committees responded with greater alacrity than their House counterparts. After much prodding by Leon Panetta (D-Calif.), who

28. For his close collaboration with the Republicans, Gramm was rewarded by the Democrats with the revocation of his committee assignments. For a study of Gramm's role in the budget battle and his subsequent punishment, see Ross K. Baker, "Party and Institutional Sanctions in the U.S. House: The Case of Congressman Gramm," *Legislative Studies Quarterly* 10 (August 1985): 315–337.

29. Greider, *Education of David Stockman*, pp. 32–34.

was in charge of the HBC reconciliation task force, House committees did respond to their reconciliation instructions, though the manner in which they did so indicates that they had not come to accept the Reagan revolution in their hearts. William Greider reports:

> Some of the Democratic committee chairmen in producing their cuts were playing the "Washington Monument Game" (a metaphor for phony budget cuts, in which the national Park Service, ordered to save money, announces that it is closing the Washington Monument). The Education and Labor Committee made deep cuts in programs that it knew were politically sacred: Head Start and Impact Aid for local schools, and care for the elderly. The Post Office and Civil Service Committee proposed closing 5,000 post offices.[30]

In response to the attempted subversion of the president's budget, Republicans on seven committees together with OMB prepared alternate reconciliation legislation. The Republicans planned to repeat their earlier success in adopting the resolution by substituting on the floor for the reconciliation legislation from those committees. The president and his men mounted a massive lobbying effort on behalf of Gramm-Latta II (as the package of substitute legislation was known). The mobilization of the public by both the administration and its interest-group allies succeeded in causing the Reagan faithful across the country to send letters and call their representatives in unprecedented numbers. The House mailroom was inundated with letters and also, improbably, thousands of pie plates, sent to symbolize

30. Ibid., p. 52. Closing post offices makes much sense for developing postal efficiency, but they are politically untouchable.

the desire of their senders that the shares of the budgetary "pie" be rearranged.

Normally the constituency for indirect benefits is in-
visible and inactive, but the size of the reconciliation
bill enabled Reagan to focus attention on it and create a
massive, clamorous constituency for budget cutting.[31]
The Democratic leadership's strategy for defeating
Gramm-Latta II was to vote separately on each committee package. The Democrats thought that if each committee's legislation was considered in comparison only
to that proposed in its place, some or all of the substitutes could be defeated. The Republicans, on the other
hand, sought a single up or down vote on the entire
Gramm-Latta substitute. In compliance with the wishes
of the leadership, the Rules Committee reported a resolution that broke Gramm-Latta into seven packages,
each with a separate vote, and also disallowed its non-
budgetary provisions—of which there were plenty. The
critical vote was on the rule. At this, the second crucial
juncture of the budget process in 1981, the Republicans
again prevailed over the putative Democratic majority.
After the Rules Committee rule was first defeated, Delbert Latta, ranking minority member on the committee,
offered a substitute rule that called for a single vote on
all the substitute reconciliation legislation, and it
passed. The House then considered the Gramm-Latta II
package en bloc and passed it.

On the strength of just two key votes—first on the resolution and second on the reconciliation bill—the Republican House minority with the assistance of the boll
weevil Democrats was able to avoid almost completely
the normal obstructionism of the committee system of

31. Phil Gramm, holder of a Ph.D. in economics, demonstrated his
understanding of this problem in an article, "Understanding the Deficit Problem," *Wall Street Journal*, Oct. 16, 1980, p. 28.

Congress and pass President Reagan's budgetary program in its entirety. By ordinary procedure, cutting a hundred or so programs, as the reconciliation bill did, would require that the administration position prevail on each of several hundred votes—in subcommittees, in full committees, and on the floor, in both the House and the Senate. In this case, a legislative majority that was not the majority party triumphed over both the committees and the majority leadership by controlling the floor.

1982

The third consecutive year of reconciliation in the budget process continued the unblemished record of budget resolutions originating from sources other than budget committees. The president's budget in 1982 disappointed the many who had hoped Mr. Reagan would make a serious effort to deal with the mounting size of the federal deficits. This budget proposal was satisfactory to no one, for not only did it project a deficit in the $200 billion range, but it required large social spending reductions just to keep it that low. After it quickly became apparent that the president's budget was useless as a guide to budget action, leaders from the House and Senate, along with representatives from the White House, met to negotiate a compromise budget. This group, known as the Gang of Seventeen, was able to agree on a number of technical issues, but it could not agree on important issues of budget priorities. After six weeks of negotiations, the summit broke up on April 28, after which both budget committees began independent efforts to craft resolutions that could pass.[32] Unlike the

32. Lawrence Barrett describes these meetings in *Gambling With History* (New York: Penguin, 1984), chap. 20, pp. 364–371. Paul Light describes the "Gang" in the following manner: "The meetings seemed to inaugurate a new form of presidential-congressional gov-

previous year, the SBC broke publicly with the president, and, on a strict party-line vote in committee, reported out a resolution that called for tax increases and smaller budget cuts than the president had requested.[33] This was a daring departure, for the committee took the lead in calling for cuts in Social Security. The president had been adamant in his opposition to any kind of tax increase, but, before voting to report, the Republicans on the committee persuaded Reagan to give the resolution his lukewarm blessing.

Vehement opposition appeared immediately. Senator Daniel P. Moynihan (D-N.Y.) introduced a "Sense of the Senate" resolution in the Senate denouncing cuts in Social Security. It was narrowly defeated and replaced by a milder condemnation that passed 96–0.[34] Following this early rebuff, the resolution came to the floor where, after a couple of days of debate, it became clear that it could not pass in its present form. Majority Leader Howard Baker called a recess, and the Republicans repaired to a caucus. There they met behind closed doors for several days and rewrote the resolution. Among other changes, they deleted the Social Security cuts and

---

ernment. The meetings were secret. There were no minutes or transcripts. All conversations were strictly off the record. The gang was free to discuss all of the options without fear of political retaliation. It became an ad hoc, month-long negotiation group, existing completely outside the constitutional system. This was not just separate institutions sharing power; this was a new kind of government body involving a single chamber of national leadership. . . . Unlike presidential commissions, the gang had considerable power to enforce its decisions inside Congress." Light, *Artful Work: The Politics of Social Security Reform* (New York: Random House, 1985), pp. 143–144.

33. Senate Budget Committee, *First Concurrent Resolution on the Budget, FY 1983*, S. Rept. 97–385, 97th Cong., 2nd sess. (USGPO, 1982).

34. Light, *Artful Work*, p. 129.

relieved the Labor and Human Resources Committee of its reconciliation cuts (at the request of Orrin Hatch, the committee's chairman, who was expected to face a tough electoral challenge in the fall). After being renegotiated in the caucus, the resolution was taken back to the Budget Committee and very quickly reported out. Committee action at this stage was absolutely perfunctory. Senator Joseph Biden (D-Del.) described the committee action as follows: "Gone were the days when we worked function by function, mission by mission, to weigh program priorities against fiscal policy dictates. As our chairman put it, the committee has 'matured beyond' that. It was all over in a matter of minutes, and the committee had adopted a plan that had seen the light of day only hours before."[35]

The purpose of the Republican caucus was to negotiate a resolution behind which all the party could stand united, in order to turn aside the expected onslaught of difficult Democratic amendments. Unless the Republicans could agree and pledge themselves to reject all amendments before taking the package to the floor, the package would come apart under the pressure of "grandmas versus tanks" amendments. As expected, the Democrats did offer various tempting amendments, but the Republican strategy worked: the Republicans were able to remain very nearly unanimous in opposition to the amendments. Only one, a James Sasser (D-Tenn.) amendment to restore cuts in railroad retirement benefits, passed. The Republicans, on the other hand, offered no amendments at all.

The twelve Republicans on the SBC were in a position neither to speak for the entire party nor to negotiate

35. *Cong. Rec.*, daily edition (May 21, 1982), p. S5869.

controversial budget packages and expect the rest of the party to follow. Instead, the resolution was negotiated in the Republican caucus itself. The key to controlling the budget resolution is the ability to assemble a majority, and that is a task for which budget committees are ill-suited.

In broad outline, House action on the resolution in 1982 nearly duplicated that of 1981. On a partisan vote the HBC reported a resolution that was subsequently defeated on the floor. Ultimately a Republican substitute passed, backed by a coalition nearly identical to that which passed Gramm-Latta II the year before. But the details of the process reveal both the inability of the HBC to exercise leadership in budget matters and the extent to which budget action centered on the floor.

Exactly as he had the year before, HBC Chairman James Jones drafted a resolution and brought it into committee; it was reported out without any Republican support. Before this resolution came to the floor, however, it became an orphan. Both Jones and the leadership backed away from it to support a different resolution sponsored jointly by Jones and the House leadership. The floor contest, then, centered not on the HBC-reported resolution, but on three substitutes: one liberal, offered by Jones and leadership; one moderate, offered by Les Aspin (D-Wis.); and one conservative, offered by Delbert Latta. The rule governing floor consideration treated each substitute amendment as equal, according none a privileged position.

Of these, the Latta amendment was initially favored to win. But discipline within the conservative coalition broke down in the amending process, and a carefully negotiated package fell apart. The problem developed when an amendment offered by Mary Rose Oakar (D-Ohio) to transfer funding from defense to social spending passed on all three substitutes. Republican disciplines dissolved on the floor, allowing the Oakar amendment—which had not been expected to pass—to win by a substantial margin. David Broder explains how this could happen:

> Up for consideration was an amendment by Rep. Mary Rose Oakar, D-Ohio, to the Republican budget Michel and the President were backing. . . . The Democratic leadership was backing Oakar in confident expectation that Michel would have the votes to defeat her, thus giving the Democrats yet another of what they called their "grandmas vs. submarines" election issues.
>
> But suddenly, more than 60 hard-core Republicans were abstaining. This surprise show of displeasure with the Reagan-Michel budget lasted until the final 60 seconds of voting. Then, 51 of the 62 "yellow-jackets," by the count of Newt Gingrich, R-Ga., one of their leaders, relented and voted with Michel.
>
> But by then the Republican leader had lost control. In the nervous confusion, with the leadership in obvious disarray, both conservative Democrats and Republicans in shaky districts flocked to support Oakar, and 11 of the "yellow-jackets" joined them. With no time left on the clock, Michel was stuck with a 228–196 vote that stripped the Republican budget of its promised Medicare savings and reduced the defense budget far below the level Reagan wanted.[36]

36. David Broder, "Yellow-Jackets Block Victory for GOP in House," *Oakland Tribune*, May 28, 1982, p. A-1.

Thus the Latta substitute, which might well have passed had it not been mutilated by a Democratic amendment, was rendered too liberal by the diminution of the defense function. After the House finished amending the three substitutes, it proceeded in one brief but decisive session to vote them all down.

Two weeks later the House again attempted to pass a budget resolution, this time with success. The HBC reported yet another resolution in the interim but not one the committee Democrats wanted to see passed. They drafted the president's budget submission into the form of a resolution, recalculated it according to CBO economic projections, and reported it.[37] If it came to a vote, Republicans would face an unpleasant choice. They could either vote against a budget resolution they found distasteful and betray their president or loyally support a resolution they found quite unacceptable. The Democratic and Republican leadership both offered complete substitute resolutions, so that the HBC-reported resolution would come to a vote and embarrass the Republicans, only if neither of the two major substitutes passed. To ensure that one would pass and that the disaster of the first attempt was not repeated, both substitutes were protected by a closed rule, giving each a single, clear vote. Thus protected, the Republicans were able to hold their coalition together and passed their substitute, 219–206.

Apart from its initial effort to produce a passable resolution, the HBC assumed a noticeably minor role: neither of its resolutions was ever in serious danger of passing. In the second round of budget consideration the

37. House Committee on the Budget, *First Concurrent Resolution on the Budget, FY 1983,* H. Rept. 97–597, 97th Cong., 2nd sess. (USGPO, 1982).

HBC completely abandoned the effort to assume a position of leadership.

1983 and After

The pattern established in the first three years of reconciliation has continued in much the same manner, although with some variation and embellishment. The SBC has been notably ineffectual, while the HBC has participated more fully, although not occupying a position of conspicuous or independent leadership.

In 1983 the SBC was utterly incapable of agreeing on a serious budget resolution and so, to enable the process to continue, reported a strictly pro forma resolution intended only to serve as a vehicle for floor amendments. The battle to pass a resolution was, in the fullest sense, floor-centered as competing resolutions were debated on the floor. On the basis of careful negotiations a bipartisan resolution, drawing most of its support from the minority Democrats, was able to pass by a margin of one vote. In 1985 the SBC began its deliberations on an auspicious note—a bipartisan vote to cut the defense function. But that cooperative spirit soon disappeared. Committee Republicans met in caucus to complete the resolution and then reported it out by a party-line vote. All this was for naught, however, as the SBC resolution was completely ignored. The crucial negotiations took place later, between Majority Leader Dole and the White House.

In 1983 the HBC recovered from the disasters of the previous two years to write a budget resolution and pass it on the floor. However, the committee did not assume a role of independent leadership. Its purpose, rather, was to negotiate a resolution capable of holding together a diffuse Democratic party. In 1984, unable to reach internal agreement on a resolution, the HBC took the novel approach of reporting two resolutions, one favored by the chair, and the other, called "pay-as-you-go," devised by George Miller (D-Calif.), a junior member of the committee. Miller's resolution, although opposed by the leadership, passed on the floor.[38] Even when the HBC has been able to pass a resolution, the negotiations leading to it center not on the House Budget Committee or its Democratic members, but on the entire Democratic party.[39] In writing the resolution, the HBC leader looks more to his party than to his committee. For instance, to assist in producing a resolution in 1983, the HBC circulated among House Democrats a questionnaire designed to ascertain their views on a range of budget issues and involved many members in the process of writing a resolution.[40]

As reconciliation was introduced and the budget process became powerful, the focus of budget activity moved from budget committees to more inclusive and more authoritative groups. Since 1980, the budget process has served as an extracommittee structure within which broad budget negotiations have taken place and by which the decisions thus reached have been implemented.

38. In 1984, a large number of complete substitutes were offered as amendments; Tim Wirth (D-Colo.) offered Reagan's budget as a floor amendment. Only Jack Kemp voted for it as it went down in humiliating defeat, 1–401. *CQ Almanac, 1984*, p. 20-H.

39. "The entire Democratic membership of the House took an active role in the formulation of the budget resolution reported by the House Budget Committee on March 21. The Democratic caucus held several meetings to discuss the budget." *CQ Almanac, 1983*, p. 436.

40. House Budget Committee, "An Exercise in Hard Choices: Policy-Alternatives," typescript, March 2, 1983. Again in 1985, under a new chairman, Bill Gray (D-Pa.), the HBC circulated the same kind of questionnaire.

Change in the Senate Budget Committee

The success of the reconciliation process has led to charges that the budget committees have become "super-committees." Such allegations can be due only to a serious misunderstanding of their role. The number of votes within a committee is a reasonable measure of the extent to which the committee itself, through its own internal deliberations and negotiations, actually wrote the measures it reports. The more votes in committee, the more directly the members of the committee participated in determining the resolution's content. When there were few votes, we can expect that the committee merely ratified a document written elsewhere and presented to it. As Table 3 shows, the Senate Budget Committee took tremendous numbers of votes in its first years of operation, rising to a peak in 1980 (FY 1981 budget). Subsequently, the total number of votes declined precipitously, to a low of four in 1984 (FY 1985). The decline in the number of votes taken charts the decline in the SBC as an independent decision-making body.

We can also see the decline of bipartisanship in the SBC. Muskie and Bellmon inaugurated the SBC on a bipartisan basis, with the committee minority participating fully and equally in deliberations and markup. Table 3 also summarizes an analysis of votes in committee, broken down according to (1) the party of the member offering the motion and (2) whether the motion was passed. Prior to 1980, more than one-third of all successful motions were offered by the minority, and more than half the motions offered by the minority passed. This evidence indicates that the committee business was conducted on a highly bipartisan basis. Beginning in

Table 3
*Minority Participation in the Senate Budget
Committee, FY 1976–1989*

Fiscal Year	Total	Majority Motions		Minority Motions	
		Passed	Rejected	Passed	Rejected
1976	26	6	14	2	3
1977	56	14	15	19	8
1978	53	25	10	5	7
1979	74	24	15	20	15
1980	137	75	23	26	11
1981	192	87	53	25	25
1982	60	23	9	7	16
1983	28	6	1	0	20
1984	43	11	6	6	16
1985	6	2	1	0	1
1986	60	14	11	16	19
1987	15	0	2	0	3
1988	16	4	7	1	2
1989	5	2	2	0	1

SOURCE: Author's tabulation from Senate Budget Committee, *First Concurrent Resolution on the Budget*, various years.

1980, when the committee largely adopted the recommendations of the leadership group, fewer and fewer minority motions were accepted. Since 1982 (FY 1983), almost no minority motions have been accepted. SBC deliberations, to the extent they deserve that term, were extremely partisan in 1982. Twenty-seven votes were recorded in committee, and on none of those involving substantive matters (as opposed to, say, votes on economic assumptions) did *any* Democrats vote for Republican proposals or *any* Republicans vote for Democratic proposals.[41] In 1983 (FY 1984) and 1984 (FY 1985), no

41. Senate Budget Committee, *First Concurrent Resolution on the Budget, FY 1983*, S. Rept. 97-385, 97th Cong., 2nd sess. (USGPO, 1982), pp. 121–135.

Table 4
Senate Budget Committee Votes, FY 1986

	Majority Motions		Minority Motions	
	Passed	Rejected	Passed	Rejected
Round One (March 5–12)	6	10	15	14
Round Two (March 13–14)	8	1	1	5

SOURCE: Author's tabulations from Senate Budget Committee, *First Concurrent Resolution on the Budget*, FY 1986.

member of the majority party voted for any motion offered by a member of the minority.

In 1984, the committee members formally recognized that the committee's character was fundamentally altered and that they no longer constituted a deliberative body. For the first time, they dispensed with the detailed function-by-function approach to markup and instead considered only complete packages. In 1985 (FY 1986) the SBC tried again to employ the function-by-function style of markup, but it was not successful. Over the first week of deliberations, as shown in Table 4, committee action was remarkably bipartisan, with more Democratic than Republican motions passing, some of them by very large margins. Mostly these votes concerned the more minor functions in the budget. Social Security, however, was too contentious an issue, bipartisanship broke down, and all the work up to that point was scrapped. The committee Republicans met in caucus and at length wrote a resolution that was then adopted by a nearly perfect party-line vote in the full committee.[42] Even though they passed the resolution, the action

42. In minority views attached to the committee report, three

was largely perfunctory, intended to fulfill the committee's responsibility to report a resolution and enable the
process to continue in a larger forum. Mark Andrews (R-
N.D.) remarked that Republicans "were voting for this
turkey to get it out of the committee and onto the
floor."[43] This is the picture of a bipartisan committee become partisan, of a deliberative body that has ceased to
deliberate. In no sense is it the portrait of a "super-
committee."

Floor-Centered Activity

A Congress in which a party caucus decides on a comprehensive budget policy that is subsequently implemented, or in which a bipartisan floor majority is able
to do the same, is not like the Congress that appears in
textbook descriptions. As members of Congress have become gradually more concerned with the budget as a
whole—which is to say, with budgetary aggregates—
they created a budget process that has enabled congressional majorities to exercise control over budget policy.
This new budget process enables them to express their
preferences, not just on the parts of the budget as the old
system did, but also on the whole. When considered as a
whole and guided by constraint, the budget becomes so
inclusive, so unavoidably redistributive in character
and thus so divisive, that the normal committee struc-

Democrats lamented that "despite all the individual decisions made
by this committee [in some sixty votes] most of the assumptions on
which those choices rest were either reversed or erased in a single
vote adopting the committee chairman's substitute." Senate Budget
Committee, *First Concurrent Resolution on the Budget, FY 1986*, S.
Rept. 99-15, 99th Cong., 1st sess. (USGPO, 1985), pp. 340–341.
    43. *CQ Almanac, 1985*, p. 447.

ture of Congress cannot possibly deal with it. Consequently, with the institution of budget control in 1980, we have witnessed the emergence of a new, "floor-centered" legislative style. Such a development was neither explicitly sought nor foreseen when the Budget Act was written or perhaps even when reconciliation was introduced in 1980. Budget committees were set up to oversee the process, but the role they were intended to fulfill, having assumed overarching importance, has been taken over by other, more authoritative bodies.

Budget politics have been floor-centered, but not in the sense that major choices are necessarily made on the floor. They are floor-centered in the sense that mobilizing a floor majority to pass a comprehensive budget resolution has become the most important action each year in Congress; moreover, these majorities do not accept the choices presented to them by committees. Rather, the resolution emerges from negotiations that involve large numbers of members. In the past, committees served as the winnower of legislation, and nearly any legislation reported by a committee has passed on the floor. Floor passage did not constitute a major obstacle to passage, except for certain highly partisan committees.[44] Congressional majorities had little power except to reject or slightly modify the decisions presented to them by committees. Once majorities were weak, and committees strong; committees are still strong, but majorities have now gained greater capacity to dominate and subordinate the committees.

44. The leading example of a partisan committee with little influence on the floor is the House Education and Labor Committee. See Richard F. Fenno, Jr., *Congressmen in Committees* (Boston: Little, Brown, 1973).

When budget resolutions are meaningful documents, initiative in policy moves from committees to whoever is able to control the floor. The politics of budget resolutions is floor-centered, not because all that is important occurs there, but because now floor control means the ability to force action, direct committees, and determine the shape of budget policy, rather than merely to halt action. Reconciliation is an "action forcing mechanism." The importance of this can hardly be overstated, for it obviates the practical veto over legislation normally possessed by committees in their jurisdictions. Increasing the power of majorities increases the importance of the floor compared to that of committees.

One might argue that budget politics have become "party-centered" rather than floor-centered because parties tend usually to organize congressional activity outside committee. I have no theoretical objection to this logic. However, although the congressional parties have taken leading positions in budget formulation, they have not been able to systematically dominate the budget process. In 1983 Slade Gorton organized a bipartisan coalition to pass a resolution, and in 1985 George Miller (D-Calif.) was able to mobilize a large group of freshman, Democratic members of Congress to pass his pay-as-you-go resolution, which was opposed by the leadership. The budget process would be party-centered if the parties were able to mobilize majorities to pass budget resolutions. Because they have not been able to do so, the question of who dominates the budget process remains open. I use the more inclusive term "floor-centered."

Moving power out of committees, to the floor, changes the character of the legislative process. Norms of universalism and reciprocity, traditional signs of civility in

Congress, are little in evidence while considering budget resolutions. Passing budget resolutions, unlike most congressional action, involves "hardball" politics. When issues are considered individually, without posing explicit trade-offs between programs and functions, members can engage in cooperative, mutually beneficial behavior. By not criticizing each other's favorite programs and by voting to fund them all, all members can benefit. Conflict in Congress can be limited by not considering trade-offs, but budgets cannot be controlled by this means. The budget process affords members the possibility of maintaining budget control, but only by destroying the internal calm of Congress, for it is nothing if not an exercise in budget choices. When considering budget resolutions, Congress ceases to be a "cocoon of good feeling," and serious conflict emerges.[45]

Change in the behavior of Congress is frequently associated with changes in its rules and organization. Structure never solely determines events, but it commonly intervenes between the emergence of majority preference in favor of a given policy and its realization in legislation. Just as the mere existence of majorities in favor of Civil Rights legislation did not assure passage in the early 1960s, the desire of congressional majorities in the 1970s to exert greater control over the budget did not suffice to accomplish that purpose. In both cases procedural barriers got in the way, and in both cases structural change had to occur before the majorities

45. Clem Miller used this phrase to describe Congress. Quoted in David Mayhew, *Congress: The Electoral Connection* (New Haven: Yale University Press, 1974), p. 79.

could win. When members demand to control the budget from the top down, as they now seem to do, they need a different budget system than that providing bottom-up control. Since 1980, members have had such a system, and, beyond its budgetary consequences, it has also changed the face of Congress.

4

Committees in a Floor-centered Budget Process

Although ambiguity surrounds the question of who in
Congress gains through the budget process, there is
little doubt about who loses. Quite simply, the relationships between the committees and the chamber have
changed, and committees no longer occupy the same as-
cendent position they once did. Over committee actions
the chamber has always possessed some measure of
power, mostly negative in character. Control of the legislative agenda has traditionally rested with the committees, and the chamber—or, in other words, congressional floor majorities—could do little but veto or
slightly modify the decision presented by a committee.
The chamber could do little to influence committee decisions and actions. Through the budget process, the
chamber now takes initiative and directs the committees' activities, intruding into the internal affairs of the
committees and diminishing their autonomy. This chapter discusses the relationships between committees and
their parent chamber and how they have been affected

by the budget process. Here I emphasize mostly the House.

Committee Autonomy and Chamber Controls

The point that the committees have been the center of the legislative process has been made and reiterated by nearly every observer of Congress. This observation is only reinforced by examining the disposition of bills in Congress. Nearly all bills reported by committees and sent to the floor are passed, the great majority of them without amendment. From 1963 to 1971, for instance, 70 percent of bills in the House and 65 percent of bills in the Senate passed without amendment.[1] In spite of occasional major floor battles over highly controversial bills, most legislation reported by committees has passed routinely. Committees, not the floor, have been the graveyard of legislation. Members of Congress introduce vastly more legislation each year than the committees report.[2] In determining their own agenda, the committees determine the agenda of Congress. Focusing on the simple fact of committees' floor success obscures a more complex relationship. Despite the power they exercise, committees have no absolute rights or prerogatives, only those allowed them by the chamber. The subordinate, dependent position of committees is underscored every time a bill comes to the floor; unless bills receive majority support, they do not pass. Com-

1. Randall Ripley, *Congress: Policy and Process*, 2d ed. (New York: W. W. Norton, 1978), p. 191. The rate of passage varied quite a lot from committee to committee, from a high in the House of 90 percent (Ways and Means) to a low of 41 percent (Science and Astronautics).

2. Approximately one-tenth as many bills are reported each Congress as are introduced. See Roger H. Davidson and Mary Etta Cook, "Indicators of House of Representatives Workload and Activity," Congressional Research Service, April 3, 1984, p. 58.

mittees that are "rolled"—or lose—on the floor are not powerful. Rejecting the work of committees is a blunt but effective sanction, the threat of which largely suffices to keep committee action from diverging drastically from the majority preference in the chamber. According to this interpretation, the high success rate of bills on the floor indicates that committees anticipate chamber reactions, not that committees are all-powerful. Studies of the two most important House committees—Ways and Means and Appropriations—argue that their floor success results from being highly attuned to the expectations and preferences of the rest of the House. John Manley reports:

> By the time the Ways and Means Committee is finished marking up a bill enough conflicting demands have been met so that, although not everyone wins or is satisfied, the Committee majority does not lose on the floor. The ultimate forms of House control remain just that, ultimate. No doubt the closed rule gives the Committee floor advantages that other committees would like to have, but far from destroying House influence on the Committee the closed rule depends for its existence on such influence. Ways and Means anticipates what other members of the House will support, compromises more than it categorically rejects, and, by being predisposed to act favorably on what House members and others desire, prevents effective demands for an open rule.[3]

Unlike Ways and Means bills, appropriations bills do not obtain the protection of a closed rule, but, nonetheless, members of the committee similarly accommodate themselves to the chamber in order to ensure the pas-

3. John Manley, *The Politics of Finance* (Boston: Little, Brown, 1966), p. 237.

sage of its bills on the floor. According to Richard Fenno, "Committee members try to meet House expectations through the content of their recommendations. By the time the Committee has reported its bills to the floor, it hopes that all the potential points of conflict between itself and 'the House' will have been settled and acceptance will be readily forthcoming. . . . It appears that the Committee does win the bulk of its House support in this fashion—by making substantive decisions that meet House expectations."[4]

Bills coming from committees that do not take such pains to produce broadly acceptable legislation are much more heavily amended. The House Education and Labor Committee is the best example of a committee that does not concern itself with accommodation to the chamber; as a result it does not exercise much power.[5]

Committees are not necessarily powerful or influential on the floor, but, by working hard at producing good legislation, satisfying affected interests, and basically meeting chamber expectations, they can maintain considerable control over important policy areas and develop some measure of autonomy from the parent chamber. Still, the power of a committee does not consist of an ability to do whatever its members like, for, as a member of the Rules Committee once explained, "the Committee on Appropriations cannot do one thing—they cannot appropriate and they cannot prevent the appropriation of money unless that is the will of the House."[6]

All congressional power ultimately resides in congressional majorities, but exercise of that power is lim-

4. Richard F. Fenno, Jr., *The Power of the Purse* (Boston: Little, Brown, 1966), p. 417.

5. Richard F. Fenno, Jr., *Congressmen in Committees* (Boston: Little, Brown, 1973).

6. Quoted in Fenno, *Power of the Purse*, p. 20.

ited, both by committee legislative initiative and the difficulty of undertaking major revisions on the floor. The major sanction available to the chamber is to defeat legislation, but this is essentially negative in character. Committees will not always get their way, but they are assured that no legislation will be undertaken in their jurisdiction except what they initiate. Procedural devices equipping the chamber to do more than veto or slightly alter committee actions have barely constrained committees. Neither the motion to recommit with instructions nor the discharge petition has been used with any frequency.[7]

Committee members—especially those with greater seniority who are thereby in a better position to benefit from their committee work—very much want autonomy for their committees. They want to be left alone to manage affairs within their jurisdictions according to their own preferences and judgments. They want to be able to set their own agenda, write legislation as they see fit, report it when they want, and watch it pass on the floor. The less the chamber interferes, the more members can benefit from participating on committees.

Increasing Committee Autonomy

Apart from the Budget Act, many changes in congressional organization in the 1970s can be understood as

7. Committee power on the floor has declined in recent years, as members have become more willing both to offer and to vote for amendments to legislation. Stanley Bach documents the increase in amendments to appropriations bills: "Representatives and Committees on the Floor: Amendments to Appropriations Bills in the House of Representatives, 1963–1982" (Paper given at the annual meeting of the American Political Science Association, New Orleans, Sept. 1–4, 1983). Barbara Sinclair finds an increase in amending action in the Senate: "Senate Styles and Senate Decision-Making, 1955–1980"

efforts to weaken external controls over committees and increase their autonomy. The Rules Committee and the Appropriations Committee in the House have both served as housekeeping committees and through their actions tended to frustrate the legislative desires of other committees. Both, incidentally, lost some of this power during the 1970s. The Appropriations Committee has tended to resist the incessant pressure from authorizing committees to increase spending, which, if unrestrained, presumably would lead to uncontrolled and irresponsible budgetary policy. The Rules Committee possessed the power to kill legislation by denying a rule; thus it could keep exceedingly controversial measures from the floor. In 1975 the House Rules Committee was made into a leadership committee and was thereby deprived of the independence that had once allowed it to keep liberal legislation from coming to the floor. The Rules Committee, now under effective control of the Speaker, does not often keep bills from the floor.[8]

The increased use of entitlements rather than appropriations as a funding device for programs is at least partly a deliberate attempt on the part of authorizing committees to circumvent the Appropriations Committee. When committees pass authorizations for programs, they leave to the Appropriations Committee the decision of how much to spend for them. Entitlements— in a sense, a merger of the authorizing and appropriat-

---

(Paper given at the annual meeting of the American Political Science Association, New Orleans, 1985).

8. Spark Matsunaga and Ping Chen list the bills kept from the floor by the Rules Committee from the 82nd to the 93rd Congress. *Rulemakers of the House* (Bloomington: Indiana University Press, 1976), pp. 171–176. After the 93rd Congress, rules changes brought the Rules Committee under the control of the Speaker, and it largely ceased to have an independent effect on legislation.

ing functions within single committees—increase the power of committees with jurisdiction over them because continuation of entitlements does not depend on action by the Appropriations Committee. As long as legislation does not pass, the program continues unchanged, which leaves the committee in a powerful position to protect the status quo.

Authorizing committees have sought to increase their control over those programs that require annual appropriations. When committees pass indefinite authorizations that instruct the Appropriations Committee to appropriate "such sums as may be necessary," they exercise control over the details of program administration but virtually none over the level of funding. Beginning in the 1950s and accelerating thereafter, committees have been replacing indefinite authorizations with annual authorizations and "such sums" language with explicit funding ceilings.[9] In addition, committees have also moved increasingly from multi-year to annual authorizations. By acting each year on their programs and by stating in the legislation the funding level they believe necessary, authorizing committees exercise more control over their programs and leave less to the discretion of the Appropriations Committee.[10]

The increase in entitlement spending and the common use of annual authorizations constituted an attack on the Appropriations Committee and its capacity to thwart the wishes of the other committees. By the mid-

9. See House Committee on Rules, *Recommendations to Improve the Congressional Budget Process*, Report of the Task Force on the Budget Process, 98th Cong., 2nd sess., Committee Print (USGPO, May 1984), p. 286.

10. "Any particular authorization is expected to circumscribe the [Appropriations] Committee's decision-making freedom." Fenno, *Power of the Purse*, p. 7.

1970s, the legislative committees in their quest for autonomy had greatly damaged the much-celebrated housekeeping committees.[11] Yet at the same time members were deliberately weakening traditional constraints on committee autonomy within the chamber, they were preparing to erect a new budget process. Eventually the budget process would prove more intrusive in the internal affairs of committees than anything that had existed previously. This result was not explicitly intended, either when the Budget Act was adopted or when the process was altered in 1980 by shifting reconciliation to the first resolution. But maintaining a floor-centered budget process necessarily entails a diminished committee autonomy.

Drafters of the Budget Act sought simultaneously to increase congressional control over the budget by vesting power in majorities, without crippling the committees. They centralized decisions over budgetary aggregates and created a mechanism for enforcing overall spending ceilings on individual committees. Control over program detail and decisions about how to allocate spending among programs and purposes within a committee's jurisdiction, however, were to remain the sole province of the committees. Not encroaching excessively on committees was important: a budget process removing considerable power from committees would not be able to pass; moreover, unless committees remain powerful, members will not pay attention to them, jeopardizing Congress's most important source of speciali-

11. The housekeeping committees are: Ways and Means, Appropriations, and Rules. The constituencies of ordinary authorizing committees are typically external interest groups. The constituency of the housekeeping committees is the membership of the House.

zation and, hence, power within the political system at large.[12]

Evidence presented in Chapter 3 demonstrates that the budget process has significantly increased the ability of congressional majorities to control the budget. Moreover, they have exploited this new-found capacity. Congressional majorities are able both to coordinate the activities of committees in a way never before feasible and actively pursue policies once beyond the capacity of Congress. But in establishing control over the budget, the budget process invades the jurisdictions of committees, deprives them of control over their own agenda, and diminishes the opportunities for their bills to pass on the floor.

Imposition of a floor-centered budget process alters the relationship of committees to each other and their chamber. Instead of doing what they want, when they want, committees under the budget process are drawn into a complex web of formal, externally imposed constraints. A schedule of budgeting events limits the use of the floor and makes committees dependent on the adoption of the budget resolution and the actions of other committees before they can bring their own bills to the floor for consideration. Committees lose control over their internal affairs, as the budget process enables the

12. Aaron Wildavsky, advising Congress on the issue of budget reform, wrote: "Without specialization, there is no knowledge, and without knowledge there is no power. When executives wish to emasculate legislatures, they break up existing committees and prevent the formation of new ones." House Select Committee on Committees, *The Annual Expenditure Increment*, Working Papers on House Committee Organization and Operation, 93rd Cong., 1st sess. (USGPO, 1973), p. 13. See also Nelson W. Polsby, "Strengthening Congress in National Policy-Making," *Yale Review* 59, no. 4 (Summer 1970): 481–497.

chamber to intrude as never before into the workings of committees. The process forces committees to undertake actions they would rather avoid and prevents them from doing other things they desire. Reflecting on the experience of reconciliation in 1981, Robert Dole, then chairman of the Senate Finance Committee, said that the budget process made him feel like the chairman of a subcommittee of the Budget Committee, not the chairman of his usually powerful Finance Committee.[13]

Committees cease to be independent agents and become parts of a closely knit, coordinate whole, in sharp contrast to the Congress depicted by Woodrow Wilson. Bills providing spending authority, when they came to the floor prior to the Budget Act, would be seen as individual bills to be evaluated on their own merits. With an overall budget policy to use as a standard of evaluation, members can now judge a bill, not only on its individual merits, but also by its consequences for deficits and overall levels of spending. An overly large military procurement authorization conference report provided an early test of the budget process in the Senate. Budget Committee Chairman Edmund Muskie and ranking minority member Henry Bellmon together challenged John Stennis (D-Miss.), the chairman of the Senate Armed Services Committee. Muskie explained that, with a procurement bill of that size, the only way to avoid "busting" the budget was to reduce spending on military personnel. According to Bernard Asbell's description, "Stennis is indignant. The cost of manpower

13. Senator Ernest Hollings (D-S.C.) attributes this remark to Dole. *Transcript of the Senate Budget Committee Markup of Omnibus Reconciliation Act of 1981,* p. 8. The transcript can be found in the office of the Senate Budget Committee.

is the subject of a totally separate bill. What does *this* have to do with *that?*"[14] The Budget Act makes connections between different bills and between individual bills and overall budget policy. Making such connections necessarily reduces the power of committees; bills are more subject to amendment and become the object of closer scrutiny than the committees prefer.

The top-down logic of the budget process is alien to the typical committee's way of thinking, which centers on programs and policies. A long-time staff member for the House Education and Labor Committee explained that, in his view and that of his chair, it was wrong to cut spending on child nutrition programs to reduce the deficit. Democratic members of the Education and Labor Committee prefer to determine independently how much they feel the different programs require, quite apart from such considerations as budget or economic conditions. The programs in their jurisdiction are too important for compromise with other values such as budget balance. Concepts such as "opportunity cost" and "trade-off" are unmentioned. Augustus Hawkins (D-Calif.), who in 1985 succeeded Carl Perkins (D-Ky.) as chairman of Education and Labor, simply denies that there are trade-offs: "You wouldn't think it if you listened to members of Congress, but the most important issue in America today is employment security. I don't accept the notion we're in a tight fiscal situation. . . . We've been brainwashed on limits, on security, but we haven't reached the limits of our growth."[15] One might

14. Bernard Asbell, *The Senate Nobody Knows* (New York: Doubleday, 1978), p. 272.
15. Helen Dewar, "Education and Labor Committee Endures Barren New Frontier," *Washington Post*, Sept. 17, 1984, p. A2.

surmise that, for the chair of each committee, the most important issue facing Congress was the issue most squarely in his committee's jurisdiction.

The budget process constrains the extent to which committees can base policy on their independent judgments. The process is intended to, and does, bring a greater variety of considerations to bear on legislation. Committees hold hearings and investigations and bring their detailed knowledge to bear on problems; the strength of committees stems largely from their program expertise and the importance other legislators attach to expertise in law making. To the extent that the budget process encourages members of Congress to base their decisions on something other than detailed program knowledge, the power of committees declines, causing members of committees—and especially their leaders—keen resentment. According to a staff member of the House Banking Committee, his chair resents having to operate under an externally imposed ceiling because, in the chair's view, "his judgments on housing issues are the ones that his constituents elected him to pursue." They did not elect him to defer to persons who know less than he does about housing. James Howard (D-N.J.), late chairman of the House Public Works Committee, contended that those who make decisions now about the budget are not knowledgeable: "The people who know the least are deciding the most." HBC members, he complains, have "never been within fifty feet of a public works hearing."[16] In 1981 the House Education and Labor Committee bitterly criticized reconciliation:

16. Dennis Farney, "Congress's Authorization Committee Chairmen Once Dictated Budget; Now, It Dictates to Them," *Wall Street Journal*, April 16, 1985, p. 64.

"The budget process . . . so weakens the deliberative and fact finding process of the committee system that its impact will be felt for many years after the effects of the spending cuts are realized."[17]

Having to operate within a relatively fixed legislative structure, with externally imposed limits, changes the position of individuals within the institution. More than he disliked not getting his way on the military procurement bill, John Stennis deeply resented the loss of prestige entailed in his bill's delay.

> Going into conference committee, pitting the strength of the Senate against the strength of the House, trying to return to your colleagues with the prestige of victory or at least a workable compromise, is difficult enough. But now comes this new complication, not only a crippling one but a demeaning one, as chairmen see it. After going through the torments of compromise, a chairman must go on bended knee to a fellow chairman—indeed the chairman of a mere babe among the committees, the Budget Committee—to ask meekly, "Will this compromise be all right? Do you approve of the new figure?"[18]

According to a Public Works Committee staff member, his chair believes that the "budget process involves a diminution of his concept of what he should be as a legislator." Coordination does not come cheaply; the price is a decline of committee autonomy.

17. House Committee on Budget, *Omnibus Reconciliation Act of 1981*, 97th Cong., 1st sess. H. Rept. 97-158, volume 1 (USGPO, 1981), p. 331.
18. Asbell, *The Senate Nobody Knows*, p. 273.

Intrusive Procedures

"Every time you turn around," a House committee staff member explains, "there is some procedural hurdle." In everything they do, the members and staff of committees find themselves constrained by the budget process; they resent it and wonder if the benefits derived from the process justify the pain and difficulty it imposes. The budget process is enormously complicated, and its success can be traced, in large measure, to its complexity. Were it simpler, the committees could readily find ways around it. But the committees find themselves enveloped by the omnipresent procedures of the budget process. The following pages detail some of the budget process's many features that impinge on committee autonomy. For each I will attempt to explain how it fits into a system of budget control and how compliance affects the committees.

Minor Irritants

To assist the budget committees in writing the resolution, by February 25 all the committees must send the budget committees their "Views and Estimates," a report on the new spending legislation they intend to report that year and on the levels of spending needed for ongoing programs.[19] Without such information, the budget committees cannot write a budget resolution, except by "pulling numbers from the sky." Participants in congressional budgeting often use this phrase to describe the idea of budgeting without knowledge of

19. Until the FY 1988 budget cycle, this report was due on March 15. Gramm-Rudman made this and a number of other changes in the budget process timetable.

programmatic consequences—a notion universally frowned upon.

The Office of Management and Budget releases the president's budget on the first Monday after January 3.[20] Immediately all committees commence examining what the president has proposed for programs in their jurisdictions. The Views and Estimates report typically takes the form of a commentary by each committee on the president's proposals. Going program by program, most committee reports explain which proposals the committee supports and which it rejects. In addition, they discuss the new intended legislation and the likely budgetary needs.

The report is not onerous, requiring only that a committee meet. Committees seem to employ similar procedures to produce the report. The chairman, either individually or, if the committee is bipartisan, with the ranking minority member, produces a "mark," which he brings into a meeting of the committee. There the members study it, offering amendments, voting on them, and finally adopting the report as a whole.

The staff director of an extremely bipartisan committee had great praise for the exercise of producing their Views and Estimates report. In that committee the report sets the legislative agenda for the year. The budget process does not prohibit committees from considering legislation not mentioned in the report but, barring

20. Before enacting Gramm-Rudman, the presidential budget was released fifteen days after each new session of Congress convened, which meant a release sometime in early February. To gain more time for its own protracted budget negotiations, Congress has been advancing the budget schedule for the executive branch. The Budget Act also shortened the amount of time available to the executive branch between the close of one fiscal year and the issuance of the next executive budget. OMB does not appreciate Congress trying to solve its problems at the expense of OMB.

emergencies, this committee will only take up legislation recommended in the report. On another more partisan committee a staff member explained to me that the report helps "focus" committee activity.

These mildly positive comments are overwhelmed, however, by more frequent and vigorous assertions that the report accomplishes nothing. No one interviewed in any authorizing committee seemed to believe that the report served any purpose in the budget process. John Dingell (D-Mich.), chairman of the Energy and Commerce Committee, testified that "in theory ceilings are to be constructed by adding up the recommendations of committees of jurisdiction. That is the reason that the committees submit the [February 25] report to the Budget Committee. In reality the report is ignored and the ceilings are constructed from CBO projections."[21] A frustrated staff member says of the Budget Committee: "I don't know what the hell they do with [the reports]." From another side comes a complaint that the report is meaningless because it comes so early in the year that the committees do not yet really know what they will be doing. But complaints that March 15 was too early did not stop the authors of Gramm-Rudman from advancing the due date by more than two weeks.

Although compiling the report is not in itself highly objectionable, members see it as a time-consuming, empty exercise that must be endured for no apparent reason. If there were a more widespread impression that the reports made a difference, they would be resented

21. House Committee on Rules, *Congressional Budget Process*, Hearings before the Task Force on the Budget Process, 97th Cong., 2nd sess. (USGPO, 1983), vol. 1, p. 330; this set of hearings will be cited henceforth in this chapter simply as *Congressional Budget Process*.

less. Dingell's remark implies that the budget committees should serve solely as adding machines. But if resolutions were written as Dingell believes they should be, then the budget process could not accomplish budget control. A budget process in which policy is determined by totaling up the requests of committees affords no capacity either to coordinate committee actions or to adopt a consistent fiscal policy.

Until 1986 the Budget Act prohibited floor consideration of any bill authorizing new spending that has not been reported from committee by May 15. The logic of this requirement was that unless authorizations were reported from committee, the Appropriations Committee could not begin writing its bills. Delay in enacting authorizations means delays in appropriations. Committees have an entire year, from the preceding May 15, to get legislation ready to be passed on time, yet some still have difficulty reporting bills by May 15. Bipartisan committees had less trouble meeting the deadline, but their more partisan counterparts, often delayed by internal disagreements over pending legislation, had trouble getting acceptable bills by May 15. About one-third of all authorizations are reported within five days of the deadline, some on the wrong side, leading observers to speak of a "term-paper mentality" in Congress.[22] In any case, Gramm-Rudman eliminated this irritant to committees.

Bills enacting new spending authority cannot be brought to the floor until final adoption of the first resolution. This requirement is logical because unless the

22. These are the results of a Congressional Budget Office study, reported in *Recommendations to Improve the Congressional Budget Process*, p. 286.

resolution has been adopted, one cannot know whether a particular bill will "bust" the budget. When Congress adopts the resolution before acting on authorizations, members gain access to a kind of information previously unavailable: a view of how a particular piece of legislation fits into and affects an overall budget policy.[23] Acting on legislation before adopting an overall policy subverts the goal of relating decisions on items to decisions on totals. Should the resolution be passed on time, this requirement poses no problem. But as the first budget resolution has become a more important instrument of policy, Congress has taken longer to reach agreement. In 1984, there was no final agreement on a resolution until October, after the passage of a reconciliation bill. Committees find delays disturbing because they tend to erode total floor time available to pass legislation. Floor time is scarce, and each year there is a crunch at the end of the session. Delays induced by the budget process only exacerbate the end-of-session scramble. In both 1984 and 1985, when there were lengthy delays in adopting the final version of the resolution, the leadership waived the rule and allowed authorizations to come to the floor before adopting the resolution, certainly undermining enforcement of the resolution.

A Major Headache—Reconciliation

Adopting a budget resolution does not suffice to implement the budget policy incorporated in the resolution. Actual spending policy results from a vast number of

23. Rudolph Penner, former director of the Congressional Budget Office, said: "What the budget process does is generate information." Pete Domenici, chairman of the Senate Budget Committee, echoes this view: "The budget process has served to educate everyone." Dale Tate, "Hill Budget Process Working to Force Economic Decisions," *CQ Weekly Report,* Aug. 18, 1984, p. 2015.

wholly independent legislative provisions, and they must be made to conform with the resolution if the budget policy is to be realized. There is a great contest in budgetary politics: will committee actions determine the budget policy, or will budget policy determine committee actions? Budget policy before 1980 was subordinated to committee autonomy, but since then initiative has shifted out of committee. The specific means by which the committees have been subordinated to an overall policy are reconciliation and points of order against bills breaching spending ceilings. Reconciliation provides control over existing entitlements while the point of order permits control over new spending legislation. These processes, intimately linked to budget control, more than any other aspects of the budget processes profoundly transgress the traditional rights of committees.

As it has emerged since 1980, reconciliation is the centerpiece of the budget process—the most important means by which extracommittee decisions are carried out at the program level—and the aspect of the budget process least liked among committees. Without reconciliation the budget process does not amount to very much because there is otherwise no practical means of translating into program detail the changes in entitlement spending agreed to in budget resolutions. In their capacities as members of Congress, they understand the necessity of having such a procedure to help them deal with large deficits. But when members consider the programs of their own committees, they seem to think the absence of an institutional capacity to reconcile spending policy with an overall budget policy a fine state of affairs. One slightly overwrought member of the staff of the House Interior Committee contended that a highly centralized procedure like reconciliation has no place in Congress, "the people's branch." He contends that Congress, with reconciliation, bears an uncomfortable resemblance to the Soviet Union. That constitutes the most extreme view of reconciliation, but, even among individuals less given to hyperbole, the process is tolerated as, at best, a necessary evil.

Inducements to members to defend their jurisdictions are powerful, to be sure, but success of the budget process as more than an "accommodating" adding machine demands that committees' grip on entitlements be loosened. Entitlements are the largest portion of the budget and the source of most rapid spending growth. Should control of entitlements remain in committee hands, with the committees of jurisdiction practically able to veto proposed spending reductions, congressional control over spending is virtually impossible.

The committees instructed to produce reconciliation savings are allowed to meet their target in any manner they choose, although the resolutions reflect certain assumed program changes. In the case of the Post Office Committee, budget resolutions have frequently assumed that the committee will meet their reconciliation targets by capping cost of living allowances (COLAs), but the Post Office Committee exercises its discretion and never caps COLAs. Likewise, a popular idea for raising revenue has been to introduce user fees for services that the Coast Guard provides to pleasure boaters, such as pulling grounded boats off of sand bars and rescuing yachters who run out of gas. However, the members of the House Merchant Marine and Fisheries Committee are implacably hostile to any such suggestion. Reconciliation instructions in the FY 1988 budget resolution charged the committee with finding deficit reductions worth $94 million, assuming that the committee would institute Coast Guard user fees. However, "in a clever turn of the tables, Merchant Marine members decided instead to apply the 'user fee' concept to a constituency less well represented in their districts: operators of foreign oil tankers bearing the American flag as they steam through the Persian Gulf."[24] The Reagan administration's plan to reflag Kuwaiti oil tankers and provide them with the protection of the United States Navy may or may not have been good foreign policy, but it came as a godsend to the Merchant Marine Committee.

The Merchant Marine user fee proposal highlights certain problems with the reconciliation process. The rules in the Budget Act governing reconciliation state that the committee-produced reconciliation legislation goes to the budget committees, which do not change the reports, but merely bind them all into a single reconciliation bill that then goes to the floor, via the Rules Committee. However unwise or preposterous the legislation a committee writes, the budget committees are not permitted to change it. Moreover, because few amendments are permitted to the reconciliation bill (too many amendments might cause the whole package to disintegrate), it is difficult to fix problems during floor debate. Reconciliation bills are express trains zooming through Congress, and what committees manage to pack into them winds up in law.

Consider the disruptions a process of this kind imposes on committees. First, they lose control over their agenda when deprived of their option of not acting. Second, on the floor their legislation is considered not on its own, but as a component of a large package, all of which

24. *CQ Weekly Report,* Oct. 17, 1987, p. 2507.

either passes or fails. Regardless of how short-sighted or ill-advised cuts in a particular area might be, they will pass with all the rest if the package as a whole passes. Finally, in practice, it seems that a reconciliation bill will always pass when it reaches the floor because it is unambiguously associated with economy. On the floor, the merits of the individual proposals recede from view, leaving as the nearly exclusive relevant consideration the amount of spending to be saved.

Committees are not forced to comply with instructions, but they frequently do so even when it entails reporting legislation they would not ordinarily favor because of combined inducements and threats. One might expect instead that committees would deny the legitimacy of the reconciliation procedure and refuse to collaborate in dismantling their programs. In the days of "legislative savings," members of Congress would first vote on the floor in favor of a budget resolution that implied cuts in their programs, then retire to their committees where they would proceed to ignore their injunction to themselves. Why have members not behaved similarly with reconciliation, sabotaging it through inaction? Such defiance can readily be imagined. Although reconciliation is said to be "binding," nothing is truly binding in Congress. Members of recalcitrant committees will not be locked up, their salaries will not be withheld, nor will their property be confiscated. If not such sanctions as these, what accounts for committee compliance with reconciliation?

Reconciliation and assumed legislative savings, two different efforts to control spending, vary in not only the rate of success but also the manner of adoption. Legislative savings, the precursor to reconciliation, was a budget committees' initiative. The policy changes incorporated in reconciliation are negotiated in larger, more authoritative bodies. The lack of deference accorded legislative savings by committees is hardly surprising when one considers the rather pusillanimous manner with which the budget committees proposed the savings. Allen Schick discusses implementing legislative savings as policy:

> Each year Congress would approve a first resolution assuming that billions of dollars would be saved by changes in entitlements and other laws. These legislative savings, however, were listed in the reports of the Budget Committees, not in the budget resolutions themselves. Hence, there was no vote in the House or Senate on these assumed savings. . . . Both the Budget Committees and the affected legislative committees preferred to assume, but not debate, the savings.
>
> The Budget Committees opted for silence because they did not want their resolution challenged as unrealistic or as a trespass on the jurisdictions of other committees. They hoped that, if Congress were to approve the resolution without tampering with the assumptions, it might be possible later in the year to push for the necessary legislation on the claim that Congress had endorsed the savings when it adopted the resolution.[25]

By not forcing the issue of legislative savings the budget committees avoided embarrassing floor defeats, but they also invited disrespect. Not demanding a floor vote deprived the requested savings of legitimacy.

Reconciliation instructions have not been surrepti-

25. Allen Schick, *Reconciliation and the Congressional Budget Process* (Washington, D.C.: American Enterprise Institute, 1981), pp. 5–6.

tious budget committee initiatives; they have been explicitly incorporated in resolutions; they have been debated and voted on by the entire chamber; and they have won. Because of the manner of adoption, reconciliation deserves and receives a far different reception among the committees than if it had been a budget committee product. The instructions are clearly heard as the voice of the entire chamber, and that makes a difference. On several occasions when I asked committee staff why their committees troubled themselves at all to respond to reconciliation instructions, they replied that they felt there was no choice. When instructed in unequivocal language to produce budget savings, committees apparently feel some obligation to comply. They prefer not to flaunt the expressed will of the Congress.

The perception of greater legitimacy alone does not account for compliance with reconciliation. Committees also fear that, if they do not respond appropriately, either the Budget Committee or the minority will draft substitute reconciliation legislation that will pass on the floor. This, of course, happened in 1981 when the Gramm-Latta substitute amendment to the reconciliation bill passed and produced far greater damage to programs than would have occurred if the committees themselves had produced more serious reconciliation legislation. A desire to maintain control over their programs thus motivates committees to meet their instructions. Democratic members of the House Post Office Committee do not like reconciliation cuts. "Sometimes we respond," a senior staff member explains, "but usually we don't." Some members of the committee believe they should not participate at all in the reconciliation process, but another, larger group is of the view that "stonewalling" would be counterproductive because the committee would lose control over their programs. By participating in a limited fashion, they can minimize damage.

Committee members must strategically calculate how little in reconciliation savings they can report and still avoid passage of a hostile floor amendment. They need not produce the full amount requested to avoid an amendment, and they never report legislation fully in compliance. But there are also vague limits beyond which they cannot go. "You have to avoid pissing off the Budget Committee" to keep them from supporting a floor amendment to a committee's reconciliation package, a member of the staff of the Post Office Committee reports. The 1982 (FY 1983) instruction to the Post Office Committee called for savings of about $3 billion or so, assuming the usual enactment of a COLA cap, but the committee reported savings of only about $200 million. Committee members calculated, correctly it turned out, that a floor amendment to limit COLAs would not pass. But it was also important that the committee report at least something; otherwise there would be no assurance that committee members would be appointed to the conference committee. In negotiations with the Senate, they ultimately did come much closer to the instruction (at least partly because House Budget Committee members participate in all reconciliation conference committees), but did so leaving the COLA largely intact.[26]

26. They reduced the COLA by half for retirees under sixty-two years old. Doing so saved money and mainly affected military retirees, who are of less concern to members of the Post Office Committee than of the Veterans Affairs Committee. The Veterans Committee had tied veterans' retirement policy to civil service retirements, so that whenever an increase was passed for civil servants, veterans would benefit also. Members of the Veterans Committee were not present at the conference and could not protect the interests of their constituents.

The manner of considering all reconciliation legislation together discourages certain kinds of tricks. If members of a committee could be sure that their legislation would be dealt with separately on the floor, they could feel relatively safe in reporting out the most outlandish recommendation—proposing to cut all their most cherished and popular programs—expecting that in a separate up or down vote, it would go down. This again is the "Washington Monument ploy." But when all committee packages are voted on together and amendments to delete individual committee sections are prohibited, then such a strategy of noncooperation cannot be safely pursued. What if the bill were to pass? In 1981 the Education and Labor Committee began to pursue this strategy but altered course upon learning that the Rules Committee would not accommodate their request for a separate vote. At the last minute the committee had to regroup and report a fresh, more serious proposal.

To maintain control over their own legislation, committees would prefer to focus more attention on the details and less on broad fiscal issues. A huge reconciliation bill such as that which passed in 1981 focuses almost all attention on fiscal issues. The policy issues involved in a bill cutting a hundred programs cannot be comprehended or discussed practically. In 1981 this was a problem for Democrats (and a blessing for Republicans) because it made possible the passage of substitute reconciliation legislation in place of the committee-reported legislation. If the reconciliation bill had been passed in pieces, the position of the committees would have been stronger, and, although some substitute legislation would have passed (probably in place of the Post Office and the Education and Labor packages), most committee recommendations would have been upheld. In 1982 the budget resolution allowed reconciliation legislation reported out of committee by an early date to come to the floor on its own, mollifying at least slightly the committees involved. Again, the threat of losing control over their programs encourages committees to comply.

Evasions

Responsiveness of committees to their chamber is limited, however; the extent of cheating in reconciliation is certainly large but, by its nature, nearly impossible to ascertain. A favorite means of producing "paper cuts" is to shift intergovernmental payments from one fiscal year to another. The "most egregious example of specious savings" was the transfer by the Ways and Means Committee of a Medicare payment from FY 1981 to FY 1982 to obtain reconciliation savings in FY 1981. The next year the committee reinserted the payment in the FY 1981 budget, producing FY 1982 reconciliation savings. In neither case was any spending reduced.[27]

The baselines from which committees cut, and from which the size of cuts are calculated, are often inflated, and the committees do not feel compelled to inform the Congressional Budget Office when the baseline is too high. Consequently an unknown but substantial portion of supposed reconciliation savings are a sham. In one case, the CBO incorrectly projected expenditures of $850 million on an aviation program for one year when, the year before, spending had been only $450 million, and there had been no committee expectation that

27. John L. Palmer and Gregory Mills, "Budget Policy," in *The Reagan Experiment*, ed. John L. Palmer and Isabel Sawhill (Washington, D.C.: Urban Institute, 1982), p. 78.

spending would rise to that level. The inflated baseline allowed the Public Works Committee to increase spending on the program by $150 million, to $600 million, and still receive credit for $200 million in entirely fictitious reconciliation savings.

Committee and Subcommittee Ceilings

An entirely different set of procedures facilitates control over new spending bills, including appropriations bills. The reactions from the affected committees, especially the House Appropriations Committee—both the most affected and the most sensitive to the issue of outside involvement in committee affairs—are predictable. Traditionally the Appropriations Committee, maintaining a very distinct boundary between itself and the rest of the chamber, has been jealous of the autonomy thus afforded. Members of the Appropriations Committee, according to an observer on the House Budget Committee, have become "psychologically supersensitive" about their procedure. Before 1974 the committee was subject to absolutely no formal coordination, and the few external constraints contained in House rules were often not observed in practice. House rules forbid appropriations in excess or in advance of authorizations and legislation on appropriations bills, but these rules have frequently been waived. The position of the Appropriations Committee was enviable, for its actions did not depend on those of other entities within Congress. Its bills, privileged under the rules of Congress, come to the floor without first going to the Rules Committee.

Once the central and dominant agent in congressional budget making, now the Appropriations Committee is just one part of an overarching, all-inclusive budget process. No longer can the committee go "its own way at its own speed," for it must heed instructions from the chamber. Furthermore, committee actions depend upon the timely completion of other action in Congress. Imposition and enforcement of a strict budget process alters the relationship of committees to the chamber, nowhere more noticeably than with the House Appropriations Committee.

Members and staff of the committee—and especially its chairman, Jamie Whitten (D-Miss.)—resent deeply that the process has circumscribed their autonomy. Whitten frequently points out that he strongly supported the Budget Act in 1974. But he believes that subsequent modifications have seriously twisted and subverted the process, so that now it is used in ways detrimental to his committee and contrary to the original spirit of the act. From the point of view of the committee members, there are several major problems with the budget process. All involve various ways that the budget process constrains committee behavior and limits its autonomy within the House. First, in recent years the resolution has not been adopted until a month or more after the deadline for adoption (originally May 15). Delays in adopting the resolution cause delays in enacting authorizations. These in turn delay markup of appropriations bills. Consequently, the committee contends, individual appropriations bills are not enacted on time, and massive continuing resolutions are required.[28]

Second, the 302(b) subcommittee allocation increases external scrutiny of committee actions and exacerbates internal conflict, which could be avoided by eliminating

28. Les Aspin disagrees and contends that the delays in enactment of appropriations bills are caused by the difficulty of enacting the bills once they have been reported from committee. See his testimony in *Congressional Budget Process*, pp. 29–37.

externally imposed ceilings. As Fenno described the committee: "Committee members treat every agency request as independent of every other agency request, thereby avoiding broadly programmatic decisions."[29] But when they must apportion the total committee allocation among thirteen subcommittees, such decisions can scarcely be avoided. One consequence has been "stretching out" the appropriations process. As the total committee allocation has become more constricted since 1980, the committee has taken longer to make the subdivision. In 1982, for instance, the committee took over a month of unpleasant and rancorous infighting before finally agreeing to the subcommittee allocation.

The Appropriations Committee members reserve their most spirited condemnation for attempts to exercise control over the size of committee bills. Over time, there has been a tendency toward using ever more sensitive, but also more intrusive, control mechanisms. Section 311 of the Budget Act allows a point of order to be raised against any bill that, if enacted, would breach the spending ceiling in the most recently enacted budget resolution. Seemingly simple and sure, the bluntness of Section 311 renders it nearly useless. The point of order can be raised only against the bill that goes over the ceiling—"the last pig to the trough." Section 311 does not allow members to discriminate between bills that are budget busters and those that are not. Regardless of how reasonable the spending levels in a given bill and how inflated the ones that preceded it to the floor, only the one that goes over the top can be stopped by a point of order. Because members prefer not to engage in mindless retaliation against innocent bills, the point of order

29. Fenno, *Congressmen in Committees,* p. 50.

has typically been waived.[30] For the budget process to be effective, it must be enforced against oversize bills, not those that come along at the wrong moment. Doing this means holding committees and even subcommittees to spending ceilings, and that entails intruding the budget process deeply into the workings of the committees. In varying degrees all committees with direct spending jurisdiction are upset by forays of the budget process into their internal affairs, but none more so than the Appropriations Committee, which more than others has a long-standing preoccupation with orderly procedure. Claiming that the budget process does not allow them to do their job, members of the Appropriations Committee have registered frequent, insistent complaints.

Committee and subcommittee ceilings can be enforced by means of a "deferred enrollment" procedure. After final passage of the first budget resolution, committees receive their full committee allocation (the 302[a]), which they must subdivide among their subcommittees. Committees then send their subcommittee allocation (the 302[b]) to the budget committee. Beginning in 1980, budget resolutions as reported from the budget committees have provided for deferred enrollment of spending bills that exceed either the full committee or subcommittee allocation. That is, even if passed by the House or Senate, such bills cannot be enrolled or sent to the president until the second resolution passes. Since 1981 there has been no second resolution, which makes the first one binding, and leaves the

30. See *Cong. Rec.*, daily edition (May 24, 1988), p. H3579, where Trent Lott (R-Miss.) details waivers of the Budget Act. Section 311 was waived fifty-seven times from the 96th to the 100th Congress (1979–1988).

offending bills without a reprieve. However, the rules can and have been waived to allow oversize bills to pass. The Budget Act specifically provides for this device, but it remained unused until the first resolution for FY 1981.[31] Gramm-Rudman increased the usefulness of the 302(b) process as a means of enforcing the resolution by allowing a point of order to be raised against bills that exceed their 302(b) allocation, thus preventing them from consideration on the floor.[32] As the subcommittee allocation becomes more nearly binding, tensions within committees increase.[33]

Deferred enrollment distinctly constrains committees. Resentment stems less from having to stay within an overall amount than from the lost flexibility. At a relatively early date in the legislative year committees specify the subcommittee division in their 302(b) report and thenceforth are held to it. Members of committees say their mission is to make informed judgments about their programs on the basis of knowledge and investigation, which includes the responsibility of determining how much money should be devoted to the different programs in their jurisdiction. Members of committees also claim that being locked into a subcommittee allocation at an early date keeps them from performing this function. If, on the basis of their expertise, they decide to add money to one subcommittee and take an equal amount

31. Section 301(b)(1) of the Budget Act. For a brief explanation of deferred enrollment, see House Budget Committee, *The Congressional Budget Process: A General Explanation*, Committee Print (USGPO, July 1986), p. 14.

32. See *Congressional Budget Process: A General Explanation*, p. 107.

33. Lance LeLoup, Barbara L. Graham, and Stacey Barwick, "Deficit Politics and Constitutional Government: The Impact of Gramm-Rudman," *Public Budgeting and Finance* 7 (Spring 1987): 95.

from another, the HBC will block the bills over the original subcommittee ceiling, even when the committee as a whole is within its overall allocation.

James Howard, chairman of the House Public Works Committee, contends that holding bills to the subcommittee allocation is inconsistent with the nature of policy making in his committee's jurisdiction:

> In the case of a committee such as the one I chair, the deferred enrollment mechanism fails completely to recognize the complexities inherent in contract authority programs supported by trust funds. . . . The Committee on Public Works and Transportation must make its spending recommendations in light of and in tandem with the Committee on Ways and Means. . . . Delayed enrollment puts a "chill" on this cooperative committee process, actually preventing committees from carrying out their most basic functions under the rules of the House. In conclusion, Mr. Chairman, delayed enrollment is unnecessary and intrudes so severely into the committee process as to disable the basic operation of the committee system.[34]

The idea of holding bills to the 302(b) subcommittee allocation outraged Jamie Whitten, who, in 1982, successfully deleted deferred enrollment from the resolution by means of a floor amendment.[35] In floor debate he argued against outside influence in subcommittee allocations. "Our committee and the other committees allocate to each subcommittee what appears to be its share of the total committee allocation in view of its situation. . . . It is very important to leave [the allocation] to

34. *Cong. Rec.*, daily edition (May 27, 1982), p. H3081.
35. Ibid., pp. H3076–3086.

the committees that work with it, that know what it is all about."[36]

Elsewhere, the Appropriations Committee categorically denies the legitimacy of binding subcommittee allocations. The FY 1983 302(b) report reads: "The subdivisions . . . addressed in this report are never ceilings and are not binding. The distribution reflected in this report constitutes only an internal guide to the Appropriations Sub-committees. Under the rules no point of order will ever lie against an appropriations bill because of the action taken by the Committee in making the subdivisions contained in this report."[37] "Our problem," Whitten says, "is that they do not let us run the internal affairs of our committee."[38] Whitten and Howard both contended their committees need a greater measure of autonomy and flexibility than the budget process allows. David Obey (D-Wis.), a member of both the Appropriations and Budget Committees, essentially agreed but also pointed out the need for deferred enrollment: "I think the problem is that both committees [Appropriations and Budget] have a job to do and by nature one committee's role impinges upon another's. In this instance I will admit it is a very close question because the Budget Committee has a very strong point in the necessity for it to be able to limit the tendency of committees to run all their own way."[39]

In floor debate over deferred enrollment, Whitten pleaded with his colleagues to release the Appropria-

36. Ibid., p. H3077.

37. House Appropriations Committee, *Report on Subdivision of Budget Totals Agreed to in First Concurrent Resolution on the Budget (S. Con. Res. 92) for Fiscal Year 1982 and 1983*, H. Rept. No. 97-669, 97th Cong., 2nd sess. (USGPO, 1982), p. 3.

38. *Cong. Rec.*, daily edition (May 27, 1982), p. H3080.

39. Ibid., p. H3081.

tions Committee from the shackles of the budget process: "Let us perform our function."[40] On this vote, Whitten won, and deferred enrollment was deleted from the
resolution. But some in Congress favor tightening rather
than lessening controls over the Appropriations Committee. Robert Michel (R-Ill.), the minority leader, "confessed a preference" for having the entire House vote on
the subcommittee allocation.[41] The FY 1986 budget resolution reported by the Senate Budget Committee represented a movement in that direction when it stipu-
lated a ceiling for the defense function and allowed a
point of order against any bill that would cause defense
spending to go over that figure.[42]

Subcommittee allocations are not cast in concrete;
but the committees want freedom from constraint, not
flexibility. Should committees decide, after first filing a
302(b) report, to shift money from one subcommittee to
another, they can file a second, updated report with
their budget committee. However, they do not like filing
the first one and like the prospect of filing another even
less. Although not terribly onerous, producing the report is time consuming and foreign to the committee
sense of legislative propriety. A staff person for one committee explained the problem: "Do you know what it's
like to go to your chairman and tell him we have to file
another 302(b) report? He looks at you like you're from
another planet!"

Appropriations Committee dissatisfaction with the
process climaxed in 1982, when budget process interfer-

40. Ibid., p. H3077.
41. See *Congressional Budget Process*, p. 277. Martin Frost (D-Tex.)
agrees: ibid., pp. 420–421.
42. Senate Budget Committee, *First Concurrent Resolution on the
Budget, FY 1986*, S. Rept. 99-15, 99th Cong., 1st sess. (USGPO, 1985),
p. LV.

ence in committee business was greatest. Since then, the committee has reached agreement with the leadership and the HBC: Appropriations can begin marking up and reporting their bills upon the adoption of a House resolution, without waiting for the adoption of a conference report. The HBC informs the Appropriations Committee of the assumptions behind the resolution; the Appropriations Committee then adopts an informal subcommittee division. An essential element of the agreement is that the Appropriations Committee agrees to abide by the informal targets. This strategy was a splendid success in 1983 when nine appropriations bills were reported from committee by June 21 (the conference report on the resolution was adopted June 23) and ten achieved final passage prior to the start of the fiscal year. Not since 1976 had so many bills been adopted on time. In 1984, external events again intruded to disrupt the appropriations calendar. The committee started early in reporting bills, but House and Senate conferees' inability to produce a final budget resolution until October compelled the use of a massive continuing resolution.

Whitten contends that detailed control over appropriations are unnecessary because—he frequently asserts—the committee always appropriates less than the president requests and always stays under its overall spending allocation. They do not follow the president's spending priorities, but they are not obliged to. Yet they continue the tradition of cutting presidential budget requests by means of clever and deceptive practices, for example, underfunding programs with mandatory appropriations in order to spend more on discretionary programs. The Agriculture subcommittee, chaired by Whitten, may be the most flagrant violator of fiscal probity. The FY 1982 Agriculture appropriations bill provided Food Stamp funding for only ten and a half months, which saved no money but only forced the passage of a supplemental appropriation to pay for the rest of the year.[43] The subcommittee in 1983 appropriated $500 million less than the administration requested for the Commodity Credit Corporation. The requested funds were to pay for obligations already incurred, so the money would have to be appropriated eventually.[44] And in 1984 the subcommittee funded increases in programs the president opposed, yet remained below the ceiling, by appropriating less than requested for mandatory programs such as Food Stamps and the Commodity Credit Corporation. Chairman Whitten freely admitted that the deficiencies would have to be made up by supplemental appropriations. Denouncing these actions, David Stockman, director of OMB, accused the committee of "accounting gimmicks."[45] The proliferation of cuts like these does not inspire confidence in the Appropriations Committee as a guardian of the Treasury and encourages further raids on the committee's domain.

The Problem of Coordination

The budget process coordinates the committees of Congress and enables them to accomplish purposes that would otherwise be nearly impossible. But Congress has found that "coordination" necessarily involves a degree of interdependence formerly all but unknown in Congress. The irritations, inconveniences, and complexities that the budget process causes for committees are more

43. *CQ Almanac, 1981,* p. 377.
44. *CQ Almanac, 1983,* p. 517.
45. *CQ Almanac, 1984,* p. 384.

or less inevitable, although not necessarily desirable, by-products of maintaining a floor-centered system of budget control. When Congress cannot get its work done within the timetable it has set for itself, the problem is not simply that the schedule "does not allow enough time."

Delay results from the absence of a stable, cohesive majority capable of using a budget process designed for majorities. With stable, ideologically cohesive majorities, conflict over resolutions would be brief, and enactment prompt. Divided party control of Congress, however, virtually guarantees that debate over budget resolutions will be sharp and ideological, as the two parties battle over big questions. When the nominal majority party in the House or the Senate has only a narrow advantage over the minority, it can have trouble passing any resolution at all. In the House in 1982, the close party balance led to near stalemate over the budget and substantial delay. The Democratic margin increased after the 1982 election, and since then the House has had less trouble adopting resolutions on time. But disagreement persisted between the Democratic House and the Republican Senate, and this caused serious delay in adopting the final version of the resolution. The return of the Senate to Democratic control in 1986 helped reduce interchamber conflict over the budget. If the budget resolution passes on time, then authorizations and appropriations can come to the floor and be passed on time.

Budgeting in the absence of stable coalitions, however, consumes tremendous amounts of time because members must form majorities to pass resolutions, and the two chambers must resolve their differences. Given the instability of contemporary congressional parties and coalitions, the schedule of the budget process does not leave enough time for Congress to pass a budget resolution and enact authorizations and appropriations before the beginning of the fiscal year. Of course, Congress has frequently, even usually, been unable to complete budgetary action before the start of the new fiscal year, but the budget process significantly worsens an already bad situation.

Direct external constraints on committee behavior, such as reconciliation and committee ceilings, disrupt committee life even more by delays stemming from interdependence. More than the normal legislative process, the budget process depends for smooth operation on the timely completion of a series of sequential, discrete steps. Delay at one point causes delay in all successive steps. In 1984 the Rules Committee Task Force reported that "while appropriations have sometimes been tardy in years when the relevant first resolution was timely adopted, during years when the resolution is adopted late, appropriations are never adopted on time."[46] The longer Congress haggles over the resolution and the later it is adopted, the more the process intrudes upon the committees and interferes with the passage of bills. Throughout much of the 1980s members of Congress frequently have complained that Congress does nothing but the budget—passing resolutions, authorizations, reconciliation bills, tax bills, and continuing resolutions.

The House Appropriations Committee and Chairman Whitten have often complained of inconveniences imposed upon them by the late adoption of the resolution. In 1982 the committee used its 302(b) report as an op-

46. House Rules Committee, *Report of the Task Force on the Budget Process*, p. 288.

portunity to criticize the process: "The uncertainties and delays associated with the budget resolution obviously have cost the House valuable and irretrievable time in considering the appropriations business of the session. . . . There is no longer adequate time remaining to preclude the necessity for a massive continuing resolution."[47] Under the budget process, continuing resolutions have become the most common means of enacting appropriations. Trent Lott (R-Miss.), the minority whip, remarked in 1985 (with some satisfaction) that "this year, because it has been so tied up with budget arguments Congress has not created a single new program."[48] Whitten draws on the same metaphor to describe the impact of the process: "We are tying ourselves in knots. We are not controlling the budget process— we have allowed the budget process to control our actions."[49]

The longer the resolution takes to pass, the less floor time there is available for other legislative action. Consequently, when the process preempts floor time, the normal crush of legislation at the end of the term gets even worse, and members and committees seek to pass their bills by unorthodox means to keep them from dying at the end of the term. In 1982 the continuing resolution in the Senate became the target of numerous nongermane amendments. Senator Ted Stevens (R-Alaska), the majority whip, explained: "The number of amendments tells me that there's general frustration among the membership. Most of these amendments are

47. House Appropriations Committee, *Report on Subdivision of Budget Totals.*
48. Trent Lott, "The Need to Improve the Budget Process: A Republican's View," in Allen Schick, *Crisis in the Budget Process* (Washington, D.C.: American Enterprise Institute, 1986), p. 77.
49. *Congressional Budget Process,* p. 312.

Table 5
Recorded Votes in Congress, 1970–1984

Year	House	Senate
1970	266	422
1971	320	423
1972	329	532
1973	541	594
1974	537	544
1975	612	602
1976	661	688
1977	706	635
1978	834	516
1979	672	497
1980	604	531
1981	353	483
1982	459	469
1983	498	381
1984	408	292

SOURCE: Norman Ornstein, Thomas Mann, Michael Malbin, and John Bibby, *Vital Statistics on Congress* (Washington, D.C.: American Enterprise Institute, 1982), p. 135; and *Congressional Record*, various years.

bills on the calendar but we haven't had a chance to call them up." Dale Bumpers (D-Ark.) added that "a lot of people see [the continuing resolution] as their last and best shot and feel that if they don't go after these things now they may not get another shot."[50]

Other indicators also suggest that the budget process may indeed bog Congress down or perhaps tie it in knots. The number of bills passed each session by each chamber and the number that become public law have shown a dramatic decline since 1980. Table 5 shows that the number of votes taken in Congress has similarly declined, to the lowest levels in more than a decade.

50. Martin Tolchin, "Senate Approves Bill to Run Government Beyond Today," *New York Times*, Sept. 30, 1982.

Table 6
Enactment of Symbolic Measures, 95th to 99th Congress

Congress	Total Public Laws	Symbolic Laws	Non-symbolic Laws	Percentage of Symbolic Laws
95th (1977–1978)	633	55	577	9
96th (1979–1980)	613	86	551	14
97th (1981–1982)	473	112	361	24
98th (1983–1984)	623	213	410	34
99th (1985–1986)	664	264	400	40

SOURCE: Author's analysis of listings of public laws in *Congressional Record,*
Daily Digest, various years.

Furthermore, an increasing proportion of public laws consists of purely symbolic measures—awarding a medal to Danny Thomas, designating a "Frozen Food Day," renaming the "River of No Return Wilderness" as the "Frank Church River of No Return Wilderness," designating "National Duck Stamp Week," to cite but a very, very few.[51] In the 1980s Congress saw fit to commemorate more official days, weeks, and months than ever before. Perhaps when legislators find opportunities to pursue more substantial legislation blocked, they turn instead to such silliness as enacting symbolic bills. Table 6 shows both the increase in symbolic legislation and the decline in the number of nonsymbolic laws enacted. While the number of public laws enacted has declined, the total number of pages of public laws enacted has not. The average length of statutes has grown stead-

51. These are public laws 98-172, 226, and 231, all enacted in 1983. *Cong. Rec.*, daily edition (December 14, 1983), D1606–1617. In 1983 there was also a "National Brick Week," on the occasion of which the Brick Institute of America presented every member of Congress with a brick, bearing the inscription "National Brick Week" and packaged in a padded, corrugated box (Kirk Brown, personal communication).

ily since the mid-1950s, from 1.8 pages per statute in the 84th Congress (1955–1956) to a new high of 9.2 in the 97th Congress.[52] Length reflects both the growing complexity of legislative issues and also, more recently, the tendency to pass bills in omnibus form to overcome a legislative system clogged by the budget process.

These indicators cannot be taken as proof that the budget process pushes out other legislative activity, as all could easily have alternative explanations. For example, the reduced rate of passing bills could be due to the conjunction of a Republican president with a split Congress and a severe budget constraint. Nonetheless, enacting legislation was not much hampered by Republican presidents Eisenhower or Nixon, one of whom labored with a split-party Congress and the other with a continuously Democratic Congress. Although it would be impossible to rule out all possible counterexplanations, it is nonetheless the case that observed changes in congressional workload indicators are, at least, consistent with the idea that the budget process ties Congress in knots.

Similarly, the presence of huge budget deficits, rather than the budget process, could account for the problems of committees. In this view, committees suffer, not because of reconciliation or other procedures, but because large deficits and stagnant revenue growth preclude the wide open legislative style most conducive to committee autonomy. Were the nation's economy sufficiently healthy to provide large annual increases in revenues, then we should expect committees to regain their cherished autonomy. Certainly, if the budgetary situation

52. See Roger Davidson and Thomas Kephart, "Indicators of House of Representatives Workload and Activity," Congressional Research Service, June 25, 1985.

were less dire, committees would be less plagued. But to argue simply that the budgetary situation increases or decreases committee autonomy ignores the important intermediary role of procedures and procedural change. Without mechanisms that enable congressional majorities to adopt and enforce a comprehensive budget policy, even huge deficits could have relatively little impact on the internal activities of Congress. Without such mechanisms there is no way to bring a generalized concern about the deficit to bear upon individual committees. In the 1967–1972 period, members of Congress were also concerned about the deficit, much as they have been in the 1980s. Then, however, a feud between the tax and appropriating committees resulted, and several times Congress passed spending ceilings that authorized the president to cut spending. Deficit worries led Congress to divest itself of responsibility over spending, but not to restrict the activities of committees. Within their jurisdictions committees remained supreme.

With the budget process, Congress is better able to exercise "top-down" control of spending, cutting programs to conform with an overall budget policy. A budget process that enables Congress to enforce a budget ceiling is, however, fundamentally incompatible with traditional committee prerogatives and power, which have necessarily been curtailed with the development of reconciliation.

Had congressional procedure remained unchanged, what would be the likely consequences of the massive deficits of the 1980s for committees? In a sense, the consequences could scarcely have been worse because even with its highly intrusive procedures Congress has not made vast strides in controlling the deficit. Congress has, however, accomplished purposes nearly unthinkable under normal legislative procedure, such as raising taxes and cutting spending in election years. In much of this, Congress—not the president—has been more "responsible," proposing and passing politically difficult measures. Without the budget process, there is every reason to believe that Congress would have acted as it did in the late 1960s and early 1970s, enacting budget ceilings it could not enforce. Committees would respectfully decline to comply, and their spending legislation would proceed unimpeded to the floor, where it might very well be supported by the same members who, hours earlier, had voted for a meaningless spending ceiling. A "free-rider" problem would prevent individual committees from initiating legislation to reduce the deficit but, without a budget process, collective action to resolve the problem would be more or less impossible.

Without procedural reform, Congress, incapable of translating into program detail its decisions on budgetary aggregates, would very likely continue enacting spending ceilings without depriving anyone. Committees would remain autonomous, but the prestige of Congress would necessarily suffer. Aaron Wildavsky argues:

> Power and responsibility go together. Irresponsibility equals impotence. Democratic legislatures frequently decline by making unreal decisions. When legislators typically authorize several times the amount of expenditure that is available to the Treasury, as has been the case, for instance, in the Philippines, actual allocation of real money is necessarily transferred to the Executive. The price of depriving no one is the inability to indulge anyone.[53]

53. Wildavsky, *The Annual Expenditure Increment*, p. 4.

In effect, members of Congress face a choice: they can retain the traditional prerogatives of committees in a legislature that, because it lacks the power to impose difficult choices, would probably decline; or they can accept a somewhat reduced position for their committees in a legislature that maintains its position within the constitutional order. Evidently they have chosen to adopt and adhere to a budget process that allows for more comprehensive budgeting while inevitably reducing the influence of committees.

5

Gramm-Rudman and the Politics of Frustration

Senators and representatives are often given to over-statement, but it would be hard to find a debate in Congress that provoked more dire warnings and more colorful use of metaphor than one in December 1985. "I pray that what we are about to undertake will work," intoned Senator Bob Packwood (R-Ore.). Representative Silvio Conte (R-Mass.) called the measure under consideration "a game of legislative chicken," Senator Daniel P. Moynihan (D-N.Y.) said it was a "suicide pact," Representative Henry Waxman (D-Calif.) a "doomsday machine," and Senator Bennett Johnston (D-La.) a "train wreck." All were talking about the same bill, formally known as the Balanced Budget and Emergency Deficit Reduction Act of 1985, but more commonly called Gramm-Rudman-Hollings (and more simply still Gramm-Rudman). This legislation provided a radical plan to balance the federal budget by FY 1991, and people were concerned because, unlike other legislative attempts to balance the budget, it seemed that this one might actually reduce spending, drastically and un-thinkingly. In brief, Gramm-Rudman called for the defi-cit to fall by equal increments of $36 billion each year until by FY 1991 the deficit was zero. Gramm-Rudman differed from previously enacted deficit reduction mea-sures in that it incorporated automatic or self-enforcing provisions. The law required the president to withhold or "sequester" spending if Congress and the president did not by other means manage to reduce the deficit to the mandated level.

Gramm-Rudman was a serious, sobering proposal. If the sequesters went through as called for in the legisla-tion, there was every reason to believe that many of the most important programs and agencies of the federal government would be greatly harmed. Much of Presi-dent Reagan's defense buildup would be reversed. Even its supporters often expressed only muted enthusiasm. One author and principal proponent, Senator Warren Rudman (R-N.H.), described the plan as "a bad idea whose time has come." The House Republican whip, Trent Lott (R-Miss.), offered only "reluctant support" for the proposal, and Dan Rostenkowski, who managed the bill on the floor in the House, stated that "technically, the agreement will not work in many respects." The sec-retaries of Defense and State vigorously opposed the plan and urged the president to veto it on the grounds that it would produce unacceptably large cuts in their departments.

Despite serious reservations on all sides, Gramm-Rudman moved with amazing speed through Congress. It began as an amendment to a debt ceiling bill in the Senate and quickly developed unstoppable momentum in both chambers. Less than three months passed be-tween its introduction and its passage by large majorities in House and Senate. Because it began as a floor amendment, Gramm-Rudman never went through a formal hearing process or committee deliberation, which meant that it received far less scrutiny than other legislation of remotely similar impact. How it would work, whether it would work, and how it would affect various programs were matters on which little information was available but that did not deter courageous legislators from mortgaging federal programs to a reckless experiment.

Congress enacted this drastic measure out of a combined sense of frustration and desperation. Throughout the Reagan administration Congress had been forced to struggle with the deficit problem. Between 1981 and 1985 Congress passed four reconciliation bills and cut many billions of dollars of spending, but the deficit problem never went away. Although Congress could be distracted briefly to work on other legislation, such as the crusade against drugs, the budget issue was always still there, lurking around the corner and demanding more attention. The march of budget measures to the floor was never-ending: budget resolutions, appropriations bills, reconciliation bills, continuing resolutions— all hogging tremendous amounts of floor time and all presenting painful choices, without ever solving the problem. Gramm-Rudman at least held out the promise of actually resolving the deficit issue.

Frequently in discussing the situation that made them vote (always reluctantly) for Gramm-Rudman, legislators would state that the failure of the budget process drove them to this extreme step. Clearly the budget process had not solved the deficit problem, but we should not conclude that an unbalanced budget is necessarily the result of defective budget procedures. Actually, the extent to which reconciliation had become a regular and accepted part of the budget process by 1985 suggests that the budget process was relatively effective at translating member policy preferences into legislation. Reconciliation and the budget process were not used more effectively for deficit reduction because, at least in part, the apparent universal agreement on the goal of deficit reduction was a mirage.

Members of Congress agreed almost unanimously that the budget ought to be more nearly in balance, but because of fundamental disagreements about how to achieve that goal it was normally impossible for a majority of Congress to agree on a significant deficit reduction package. These difficulties served as the principal impetus behind enacting the Gramm-Rudman-Hollings balanced budget law in 1985 and then again in 1987 after its enforcement mechanism was struck down as unconstitutional. Its proponents viewed this law as a means of encouraging members of Congress and the president to be more willing to compromise. To the extent that it did encourage compromise, Gramm-Rudman would make the reconciliation process more useful than ever before by providing the best and perhaps only way of implementing compromise agreements.

It was a clever and intuitively appealing idea, but Gramm-Rudman succeeded at forcing neither negotiations nor compromise. In early 1986 no effort was made to stop automatic cuts, and in 1987 Congress and the president would have allowed the automatic cuts to occur again if not for the external shock of a stock market crash. The effective functioning of the budget process is largely premised upon the existence of stable majorities in agreement on budget policy. Without such majorities little can be done. The experience of Gramm-Rudman suggests that efforts to force either compromise or majority use of the budget process are unlikely to succeed.

Many original supporters of the Budget Act assumed that when members of Congress were forced to vote on the size of the deficit, they would have no choice but to reduce the size of the deficit, for if they did not, angry voters would remove them from office. Things have not worked out as expected. Evidently, members of Congress can vote for towering deficits and continue to be reelected. The budget process does encourage a greater degree of consistency in individual behavior, for a majority of members of both chambers must vote for a budget resolution that stipulates the size of the deficit. But if the electorate is not inclined to vote against representatives who support large deficits then the budget process does not help to exert much downward pressure on deficits.

Cost of Deficits Appears Low

Why has the necessity of voting on the size of the deficit not curbed deficits? Public opinion and electoral pressure have not caused balanced budgets to break out at least in part because of asymmetries in public opinion. The public supports balancing the budget, but it also, according to polls, supports nearly every program in the budget. Moreover, opposition to program cuts is generally more intense than support for cuts. For example, a well-funded lobbying effort supports government subsidies to beekeepers, who are few in number, although a vast number of people pay through their taxes for beekeeping without receiving any direct benefit. But no one in particular wants to get rid of the program because it does not hurt anyone in particular. The cost is spread so thinly over the tax-paying population: no one is noticeably hurt, and no one finds it worthwhile to mobilize a campaign against beekeeper subsidies.[1] This asymmetry exists more generally as well.

There is specific opposition to almost every possible budget cut because all such budget cuts directly and significantly hurt some probably well-organized group. A budget deficit, however, hurts no one directly. Its cost is difficult to perceive because it is so widely distributed, both across the population and over time. If the $200 billion deficits of the Reagan era had plunged the nation into a depression, caused widespread unemployment or inflation, then the political support for deficit reduction would be stronger. But because the deficits coincided with a period of strong economic growth and low inflation, they appeared virtually costless.

Budget Balance a Low Priority

Balancing the budget is everyone's third priority, but nobody's first. Although President Reagan frequently voiced support for the goal of balancing the budget, as have nearly all members of Congress from both parties, there is reason to question their commitment to that goal. Virtually all politicians rank some spending program above deficit reduction and are unwilling to cut their favored program to achieve deficit reduction. In fact, for President Reagan, and probably most members of Congress, budgetary balance was probably at best a third priority.

When President Reagan said that he would not bal-

1. See *CQ Weekly Report*, April 30, 1988, pp. 1149–1152.

ance the budget "on the backs of taxpayers" by increasing taxes, he indicated that he ranked balancing the budget as a lower priority than maintaining low tax rates. When he argued that defense should not be cut to reduce the deficit, he stated implicitly that for him defense ranked above deficit reduction. Nearly everyone has some program or component of the budget that he or she would not reduce in order to lower the deficit—Social Security, agriculture, housing, food stamps, veterans, or whatever. Many representatives—perhaps all—regard a cut in their favorite program as worse than having a large deficit.

Moreover, nearly everyone believes that the way to balance the budget is to cut the programs that benefit constituencies other than one's own. By this means each member of Congress could probably produce a balanced or nearly balanced budget that he or she could support. Liberals might raise taxes and cut defense. Conservatives would cut various social programs. In arguing for the adoption of a controversial reconciliation bill in 1987, Representative William Gray (D-Pa.), chairman of the House Budget Committee, addressed this issue: "There are, Mr. Speaker, 535 members of Congress; and I might add, there are probably 535 deficit reduction plans. However, my friends and colleagues, we can only implement one."[2] The same can be said as well of budget resolutions. But neither liberals nor conservatives, nor any other homogeneous faction in Congress have a clear majority; only by compromising may progress against the deficit be made. According to Gray, "There is always some pain, and none of us will be completely satisfied, but I urge you to remember tonight when you vote on

2. *Cong. Rec.*, daily edition (Dec. 21, 1987), p. H11967.

this reconciliation package that it is the one package that can be implemented, signed into law, and receive bipartisan support."[3] Cutting the budget requires that different factions accept cuts in their favorite programs in exchange for deficit reduction. Throughout the 1980s the willingness to make such exchanges has been severely limited.

The only cost of not compromising is that the deficit continues to be large, but that is something all parties seem able to live with. Because deficits are only somewhat unpopular with the public but program cuts are extremely unpopular with beneficiaries, the prudent legislator prefers to tolerate large deficits than to impose costs on vocal constituencies.

As deficit reduction proposals make their way through the legislative process—from committee, to the floor, to the conference, to the president—controversial provisions are deleted in an effort to garner more votes. The tasks of both assembling a majority in the House or the Senate behind a resolution and obtaining the agreement of the other chamber and the president thus mean a gradual scaling down of the magnitude of deficit reduction. Deficit reduction proposals that begin very ambitiously in committee are trimmed at each stage until, when they finally pass, they are significantly diminished. Because members care more about protecting programs than about reducing the deficit, the price of obtaining their support is deleting some reduction or another. Thus, by the time each member of the majority needed to pass the bill has extracted his or her price, the package is unimpressive.

In 1981 comprehensiveness in budgeting aided efforts

3. Ibid.

to reduce spending, but in other years it has not. Fragmentation was widely blamed for congressional inability to control spending prior to the Budget Act, yet various observers have noted that comprehensiveness does not necessarily hold spending down.[4] When members of Congress place spending or deficit reduction as a top priority and are willing to reduce their own favorite programs to achieve such reductions (provided others will do likewise), then comprehensiveness will assist by allowing members to ensure that the burden of reductions will be borne more or less equally. But if an individual is primarily concerned to protect a particular program from cuts, then packaging cuts together will make him less rather than more likely to support reductions. Suppose a representative supports defense reductions but cannot under any circumstance support the limitation of Social Security COLAs. Although he can vote for a separate bill enacting defense cuts, he must vote against a bill that packages defense cuts with curtailing the COLAs.

Nearly endless wrangling over the budget in 1985 revealed clearly that, despite constant complaints about the deficit, the commitment to deficit reduction was minimal. For the White House, protecting the defense budget and low tax rates obviously ranked above deficit reduction; for the Democrats in the House, protecting domestic spending was a higher priority than deficit re-

4. Allen Schick states that "an omnibus process can lead to higher spending by expanding the scope of interests that have to be satisfied." See Schick, *The Whole and the Parts: Piecemeal and Integrated Approaches to Congressional Budgeting*, Committee Print, House Budget Committee (USGPO, February 1987), p. 57. John Ferejohn and Keith Krehbiel also argue that under certain circumstances the use of comprehensive budgeting leads to higher rather than lower spending. "The Budget Process and the Size of the Budget," *American Journal of Political Science* 31 (May 1987): 296–320.

duction. Republican leaders in the Senate seemed truly committed to deficit reduction; that is, they were willing to accept defense reductions and some tax increases to reduce the deficit, if the House would support domestic cuts. Ultimately, the White House sold out the Senate by reaching a separate agreement with the House to avoid both defense and domestic cuts, and tax increases. It was, in essence, an agreement to protect all the beloved programs by keeping the deficit high.

Having lost so badly in the presidential election in 1984, Democrats permitted the Republican Senate to take the initiative in passing a budget resolution in 1985. Although the Senate remained under Republican control after the 1984 election, passing a resolution promised difficulty because twenty-two Republican senators first elected in 1980 would be up for reelection in 1986 and would consequently hesitate to back a resolution that called for big cuts in popular programs. The SBC Republicans met frequently in caucus in an effort to put together a palatable package, but they mostly succeeded in writing a resolution that even its authors were reluctant to embrace. This resolution, called a "turkey" by one supporter, would require a freeze on domestic spending programs, eliminate any Social Security COLAs for the year, and provide for no real growth in defense. These were controversial proposals, bound to anger both the president and other conservatives for cutting defense spending and the liberals for cutting Social Security.[5]

The proposal's authors evidently hoped that liberals and conservatives would be able to support a proposal that gored both liberal and conservative oxen. Instead

5. *CQ Weekly Report*, March 16, 1985, pp. 475–478.

both liberals and conservatives, including the president, denounced the plan. A series of talks with the White House ensued, resulting in an agreement between the White House and Senate Republicans on a revised budget proposal restoring part of the COLA, providing for 3 percent real growth in defense, and calling for the outright elimination of a number of domestic programs. In late April, majority leader Bob Dole brought this package to the floor where it collapsed under the pressure of amendments. Republicans joined Democrats to pass amendments restoring full Social Security COLAs, cutting defense, and restoring funds to Medicare and Medicaid. At the end of what must have been a very frustrating day, Dole assured reporters that the damage was not permanent. "We'll put it all back together, like Humpty-Dumpty."[6] However, unlike all the king's horses and all the king's men, Dole could put it together again. True to his word, a week and a half later he brought the budget resolution to the floor again and offered a substitute amendment to the previously amended document. The substitute was very close to the original SBC budget proposal, calling for no Social Security COLA, a defense freeze, and numerous program terminations. Dole lobbied hard to get nervous Republicans to stand behind the substitute, which they did with few exceptions. Senator Pete Wilson (R-Calif.), recovering from surgery, was carried on a stretcher into the Senate chamber to cast his vote, and Vice President George Bush broke a 49–49 tie.[7] For Senate Republicans, on this vote at least deficit reduction emerged as a top priority.

Under firm Democratic control, the House had no trouble passing a budget resolution. Their resolution

6. *CQ Weekly Report,* May 4, 1985, p. 817.
7. *CQ Weekly Report,* May 11, 1985, pp. 871–874.

passed shortly after the Senate adoption of a resolution and matched the magnitude of deficit reduction in the Senate proposal but by markedly different means: the House resolution allowed a full Social Security COLA and cut defense more deeply than the Senate resolution.

The conference committee quickly bogged down when neither side would agree to significant compromises. The Democrats intended to use Social Security as a campaign issue in the 1986 election so the House conferees naturally opposed any reduction in the COLA which would erase an important distinction between the two parties and sacrifice a potent electoral issue. Senate Republicans would give no ground on defense, particularly if the House would give none on the COLA issue. After a month of fruitless negotiations, the conference broke up on June 25.

Two days later, amidst dire prophecies about the possible demise of the entire budget process, the Senate conferees countered with a new proposal, one that put taxes on the table for the first time that year. House conferees immediately welcomed this gesture as a positive sign. The Senate conferees, who acted on their own initiative without the blessings of either the president or the Senate leadership, evidently hoped that if the Senate showed a willingness to raise taxes then the House would agree to the COLA cuts.

Whatever promise the new Senate proposal might have held for breaking the deadlock was quickly destroyed by President Reagan, who was evidently disturbed by the prospect of a tax increase and a defense cut. At a White House cocktail reception for the House leadership, President Reagan and Speaker O'Neill reached a separate agreement on a budget "framework."

In a remarkable display of concerted indifference toward the deficit, Reagan and O'Neill agreed to (1) forego tax increases, (2) accept the higher Senate defense spending level, and (3) not cut the Social Security COLA. This agreement appears to have resulted from a mutual recognition that the pursuit of deficit reduction threatened programs they valued more, so they agreed to protect their favorite programs and eschew deficit reduction. Representative Jack Kemp (R-N.Y.), the presidential aspirant who untiringly supported low tax rates, reportedly convinced the administration to accept the House position on Social Security in order to avoid tax increases. In addition, sixty-seven House Republicans urged Senate Republicans to give up their insistence on COLA cuts; they did not want their party associated in the minds of voters with Social Security cuts. One may question the political sagacity of the Senate Republicans, who had voted in favor of Social Security cuts and whose conferees had raised the possibility of tax increases, but scarcely their commitment to deficit reduction.

The Reagan-O'Neill framework produced a major defeat for the cause of deficit reduction and a personal embarrassment for Bob Dole, who had led the fight against the deficit and urged reluctant Republicans to vote for his resolution. They had done so, at risk to their political careers, and now their president had betrayed them by "caving in on the COLA issue."[8] The deal provoked anger and frustration among Republicans in the Senate. Dole accused Reagan of "surrendering to the deficit." "If the President can't support us, he ought to keep his mouth

8. *CQ Weekly Report*, July 13, 1985, p. 1357. These are Bob Michel's words.

shut," opined Charles Grassley (R-Iowa), who was up for reelection in 1986 and who had voted for the COLA cuts. "That [the framework] was not an agreement of the 50 guys who jumped off a cliff over here," said Alan Simpson (R-Wyo.), in reference to those who voted for the COLA cut. Some Democrats were disturbed by the behavior of their leaders. Representative Mike Lowry (D-Wash.) complained that "O'Neill and Wright were so stuck on COLA's, they would give away the world for COLA's."[9]

With the Speaker of the House totally opposed to COLA cuts for Social Security and the president utterly against tax increases, could there be any hope for deficit reductions? Was there nothing to do other than wait for the election of a new president or a new Congress? At this point, when all other opportunities seemed to have been exhausted, Gramm-Rudman appeared on the scene.

The Invention of Gramm-Rudman-Hollings

Gramm-Rudman-Hollings (GRH), or just Gramm-Rudman, was invented in the wake of the absurd con- . clusion to the 1985 debate over the budget resolution, a debate that must have fully convinced any remaining doubters that the desire to reduce the deficit was not sufficient to encourage Congress to effectively use the budget process.

Since first entering Congress in 1979 Phil Gramm has been an ardent warrior against government spending and the deficit—first as a member of the House and then

9. Ibid., p. 1358.

since 1985 as a senator. Gramm achieved an extraordinary degree of notoriety and influence for a representative of such limited experience through his cosponsorship of the Gramm-Latta I and Gramm-Latta II substitutes in 1981. Gramm and then majority leader Jim Wright introduced H.R. 1981 to require the president to "sequester" federal spending to meet legislated deficit targets. This bill died a quiet death in the 97th Congress but rose from the grave four years later to terrorize Washington.

By October 1985 the Treasury Department would have borrowed nearly all the money it could borrow under existing statutory authority, so when Congress adjourned for an August recess members knew that soon after their return the Senate Finance Committee would have to prepare a bill to increase the federal debt ceiling and allow the Treasury to continue financing the relentless federal deficit. Debt ceiling bills are seldom easy to pass, but this one would be particularly difficult as it would raise the ceiling to over $2 trillion. Just three years before, in 1982, the ceiling broke the $1 trillion mark for the first time. Doubling the nation's debt in such short order was a record to neither take pride in nor run for reelection on; it only magnified the natural reluctance of the Senate to vote for a debt ceiling increase. Yet however much senators dreaded having to vote for the bill, it had to be passed; otherwise the government could borrow no more, throwing the government into chaos.[10] Given the dire consequences that

10. Unlike most observers, Senator Steven Symms (R-Idaho) questioned the status of the debt ceiling bill as "must" legislation. He proposed a defeat or presidential veto of the debt bill as a means of reducing spending. "If Congress chose to raise the debt ceiling, he [the president] vetoes it. . . . If . . . he is not allowed to borrow . . . he

would follow their failure to pass, debt ceiling bills "and the equally 'must pass' continuing resolution are traditional vehicles for a wide variety of initiatives on the part of enterprising senators"[11]—of whom Phil Gramm was certainly one.

Taking advantage of the situation, Senators Phil Gramm, Warren Rudman (R-N.H.), and Ernest Hollings (D-S.C.) offered their deficit reduction proposal as an amendment to the debt ceiling bill on September 25, 1985. A combination of factors—the frustrations from the previous months of largely fruitless efforts to cut the deficit and the anxiety surrounding the debt vote—contributed to a rush of support for the amendment. It would be far easier for a senator to explain to constituents a vote for a $2 trillion debt bill if it was also a budget balancing bill. The speed with which Gramm-Rudman developed support was startling. This piece of legislation promised fundamental changes in public policy yet entered the Senate agenda without the benefit of committee hearings, deliberations, or any kind of systematic expert consideration. Within little more than a week Robert Dole had embraced the concept and offered a version of Gramm-Rudman as an amendment to the debt bill. After another week the Senate had adopted the amendment. Equally startling was the breadth of the support enjoyed by Gramm-Rudman. The amendment

---

would be in a position to say he was responsible to establish priorities of spending and put the government on a cash basis overnight, which might mean furloughing workers, reducing the pay of federal workers, freezing pay. . . . I think a prudent position for the President would be to take a look at this." No other senators endorsed Symms's approach. *Cong. Rec.*, daily edition (Oct. 3, 1985), p. S12576.

11. This description of the debt bill is from Harry Havens, "Gramm-Rudman-Hollings: Origins and Implementation," *Public Budgeting and Finance* 6 (Autumn 1986): 9.

passed on October 9 by a bipartisan vote, 75–24, with the support of Ted Kennedy (D-Mass.), Carl Levin (D.-Mich.), and other liberals not known for their attacks on government.

The Speaker of the House, the chair of the Ways and Means Committee, and other influentials within the House did not support Gramm-Rudman and would have preferred a "clean" debt bill. But a quick reading of the sentiment of the House showed strong support for Gramm-Rudman and convinced them that an effort to scuttle it would fail. Consequently House leaders bent their efforts toward producing a more workable, less destructive version. For the next two months House and Senate conferees sought to rewrite the Senate-passed measure, which even its advocates conceded was badly written and probably incapable of achieving its purposes.[12] Meanwhile the Treasury Department struggled against time and the debt ceiling, trying to keep the government going until Congress managed to raise the debt ceiling.

On December 6, the conferees announced an agreement, which was quickly adopted by both chambers. President Reagan signed the bill December 12. The principal features of the conference agreement were a fifty-fifty division of sequesters between domestic and defense spending, extremely limited presidential discretion in allocating cuts (except in the defense area in the first year), and the complete or partial exemption of many programs from sequestration. The agreement required that the budget be balanced by FY 1991.[13]

12. *CQ Almanac, 1985*, pp. 467–468.
13. The schedule of maximum allowable deficits was: FY 1986—$171.9 billion; FY 1987—$144 billion; FY 1988—$108 billion; FY 1989—$72 billion; FY 1990—$36 billion; FY 1991—no deficit!

The Logic of Gramm-Rudman

Gramm-Rudman embodies a simple idea. When enacted in both 1985 and 1987, it established a series of maximum deficit levels, descending in equal annual increments to zero, and called upon the president to withhold sufficient funds to prevent the target deficit from being exceeded. The first version introduced in the Senate gave the president great discretion in allocating the cuts, but as the proposal advanced various amendments gradually circumscribed the president's authority. The form of Gramm-Rudman finally enacted in 1985 left the president with virtually no discretion. Distrusting the judgment of the executive branch, Congress established strict rules in the legislation to govern the sequester process.

First, many programs were totally exempt from the cuts while others were subject to limited cuts. The most important of these were Social Security and interest on the federal debt, but others were excluded as well, such as food stamps, Aid to Families with Dependent Children, and other programs mostly providing benefits to the poor.[14]

The second rule required that half the reductions

14. Other totally exempt programs include: veterans' compensation, veterans' pensions, earned income tax credit, child nutrition, women, infants and children program (WIC), various federal agencies such as the TVA, Indian claims, and so on. Gramm-Rudman also established a category of programs characterized as "Automatic Spending Increases" (ASI) which are entitlement programs with automatic adjustments for inflation. For these programs, only the regularly scheduled increases are subject to sequestration. See Senate Budget Committee, *Gramm-Rudman-Hollings and the Congressional Budget Process: An Explanation*, 99th Cong., 1st sess., Committee Print (USGPO, December 1985) for a listing of the programs that fit into various categories.

come from the defense side of the budget and the other half from everything that remained.

Third, in allocating the cuts, all programs that were not either (a) exempted from cuts or (b) subjected to only limited cuts must be reduced by a uniform percentage. That is, the president could not decide to reduce some programs by a greater percentage in order to grant others a measure of relief. The weight of the cuts had to be allocated equally across programs.[15]

A discussion of the technical provisions of the deficit reduction plan can never fully convey the potential horrors of Gramm-Rudman. Balancing the budget by means of sequesters would threaten the health and effectiveness of whole departments, agencies, and programs of the federal government. At the time GRH was passed, the federal deficit for FY 1986 was expected to be around $220 billion. According to GRH, then, $110 billion would have to be cut from both the domestic and defense budgets by FY 1991.

Consider first the domestic side of the budget. Total outlays for FY 1986 were expected to be about $723 billion. Most of that was exempted from cuts in one way or another—$202 billion in Social Security, $137 billion in interest, $61 billion in various low income programs, $48 billion in programs with automatic increases, $87 billion in other programs with various special rules, and so on. According to estimates of the Brookings Institution the total of domestic outlays subject to the full percentage reductions was $203 billion, and the total of all

15. For an excellent explanation of the rules governing sequestration and an account of how the General Accounting Office implemented the first sequestration in early 1986, see Havens, "Gramm-Rudman-Hollings," pp. 4–24. Havens is assistant comptroller general of the United States.

unprotected domestic and defense outlays combined was $478 billion. Brookings also estimated that deficit reductions of $176 billion would be required to satisfy Gramm-Rudman.[16] For the entire deficit reduction to occur through sequestration would mean an utter disaster for the unfortunate agencies subject to percentage reductions.

Negotiations at Gunpoint

In debate over the proposal, its supporters always resented the emphasis their opponents placed upon the destructiveness of the sequesters. The purpose of the plan, they explained again and again, was not to balance the budget by means of automatic cuts—which they agreed would be destructive—but to encourage an end to the political stalemate that had prevented progress against the deficit in the previous several years. The purpose of Gramm-Rudman was to change fundamentally the nature of the budgetary debate. Without it the result of a failure to enact a deficit reduction package merely continued the status quo—large deficits. With Gramm-Rudman the consequence of no agreement on how to reduce the deficit is frighteningly large cuts in programs, mindlessly applied. The automatic cuts were to scare Congress and the president into passing legislation satisfying the deficit targets. Representative Leon Panetta (D-Calif.) explained: "The theme in what we did was to make this thing so irrational, so ugly that it works as a club."[17] The threat of their favorite programs

16. Henry Aaron et al., *Economic Choices 1987* (Washington, D.C.: Brookings Institution, 1986), pp. 54–64; in particular, see Tables 3-1, 3-2, 3-3, and 3-4.

17. Panetta's comments were quoted by Mel Levine (D-Calif.) in the *Cong. Rec.*, daily edition (Dec. 11, 1985), p. H11891.

being beaten to death by "Grammbo" would force Congress and the president to face up to the deficit problem, or so the proponents argued.

Many members of Congress pointed out the political stalemate in Congress and the unwillingness of legislators to cut programs in exchange for deficit reduction. Gramm-Rudman, they believed, would put an end to this. According to Representative Dick Cheney (R-Wyo.),

> At present when we sit down under existing law and negotiate over the budget, there are five items on the table: Defense, domestic spending, Social Security, taxes, and the deficit. The President always takes defense off the table; congressional Democrats always take domestic spending off the table; everybody takes Social Security ... and taxes off the table. So the only thing to negotiate over is the deficit. What Gramm-Rudman does is to change that process. Gramm-Rudman takes the deficit off the table first and says to the Congress and the President that in the future, "When you put a budget together, you have to negotiate on those four other items."[18]

Leon Panetta provided a similar diagnosis:

> We are in a logjam; everyone acknowledges that. ... We know where the answer is. ... We have got to limit defense spending, we have got to limit entitlements and we have to raise revenues to pay the bills. Those three have to be put together if you are really serious about dealing with the deficit. But nobody wants to move; nobody wants to move.[19]

18. Ibid., p. H11879.
19. Ibid., pp. H11883–11884.

Panetta contended that Gramm-Rudman would break apart the logjam. Representative Jim Jones (D-Okla.), a former Budget Committee chairman, commented, "We need a new mechanism which will force the Congress and the President to face the harsh realities of our current economic crisis ... and put an honest deficit-reduction package on the table."[20] Confronted by the possibility of automatic cuts that would endanger valued programs on both the domestic and defense sides of the budget, the president and members of Congress from both parties would become much more willing to negotiate and compromise.

Democratic supporters of Gramm-Rudman sought to force upon the president a terrible choice—between allowing the sequesters to go through and have his defense buildup torn down or agreeing to tax increases as a way of avoiding the sequesters. Neither result would be satisfying to a president whose two proudest achievements were cutting taxes and increasing the defense budget. Jack Kemp agreed with the Democratic interpretation of Gramm-Rudman and opposed it for the reasons they supported it: "This enforced deficit reduction mechanism will ... impose draconian budget cuts in needed defense programs, and add enormous pressure on President Reagan to accept tax increases. In short, this plan threatens the entire Reagan revolution."[21] But Republicans could hope that the threat of large domestic cuts would make the Democrats face up to the need to exercise greater control over entitlements. The consensus among the supporters was that threatened automatic cuts would force negotiations; no supporter seems to

20. Ibid., p. H11887.
21. Ibid., p. H11900.

have favored the sequesters as a means of balancing the budget.

Some opponents, notably Bennett Johnston, disputed the typical view that GRH would force the president to the bargaining table. Johnston contended that the president, unalterably opposed to tax increases, would be unwilling to negotiate away the most significant achievement of his presidency.

> Now, you say, "Well, yes, [the automatic cuts are] a train wreck but the Congress can avoid the train wreck by doing something else." Well, by doing what? By getting together with the President and cutting $50 billion out of this budget? ... Why, the President said he is against raising taxes and he is against cutting the defense budget. So just where is this meeting of the minds going to come together ... ? Who thinks the President is going to get together with us that quickly? Why, if he does, he is going to have to back up not on one statement ... [but] on his whole political career, on the theme of his Presidency.

Could Gramm-Rudman force a consensus? Nobody knew for sure, but in passing the legislation they gambled that it would.

Sequestration in 1986

More concerned as they are with the next election than the one following it, members of Congress tend to discount the future very heavily, and this makes it easier to vote for budget reductions scheduled far off in the future. The original budget balancing plan submitted by Phil Gramm and his colleagues did not provide for any sequestration in the first year after its enactment. Sequestration would not take place until after the 1986 election, that is, not until after the twenty-two Republican senators newly elected in the Reagan surge of 1980 had faced their first reelection challenge. In negotiations with the Senate, House conferees adamantly insisted that if balancing the budget was good, balancing it sooner was better. They refused to go along with postponing Gramm-Rudman and succeeded in scheduling the first deadline for reductions for spring 1986.

Economic and budgetary projections in early January 1986 estimated that the deficit for the year would be approximately $220 billion, far in excess of the maximum allowable deficit of $171.9 billion. Under normal Gramm-Rudman rules, about $38 billion would have been cut from the deficit,[22] but special rules for FY 1986 effectively limited the reduction in that year to $11.7 billion.[23] Technically Congress had the option of preparing legislation to narrow the deficit gap by $11.7 billion and thus avoid the automatic cuts. But Congress had not yet passed the reconciliation bill from the previous year, and members were so tired and battered from enacting Gramm-Rudman that no one had any stomach for trying to pass another budget-cutting bill. The sequester was allowed to proceed uninterrupted. On February 1 the president issued the sequester order, effective March 1. The real test of Gramm-Rudman would have to wait.

22. A deficit of $220 billion was $48 billion over the maximum allowable deficit. The normal rules permitted an excess of $10 billion, so the total reductions would have to be $38 billion; half of that would come from defense and half from domestic.

23. See *Gramm-Rudman and the Congressional Budget Process*, App. X, pp. 28–29, for a description of the special rules governing the FY 1986 sequester.

Nullification and Reenactment

The most ticklish issue in designing the final Gramm-Rudman compromise was establishing a mechanism to "trigger" the sequester process and determine when deficit targets were not met. First, the trigger had to be beyond the immediate control of Congress. If Congress were responsible for initiating sequesters, then Congress would also have the power to terminate them, which it presumably would always do. Some agent outside Congress had to be responsible for beginning the process. Second, the trigger had to be beyond the immediate control of the president and the Office of Management and Budget because members of Congress did not trust the executive branch. As Harry Havens explains, "the level of details in the rules is a reflection of mistrust of the executive branch on the part of both the House and the Senate. Nowhere is this distrust more evident than in the structure of the trigger mechanism. Congress was flatly unwilling to leave control of this powerful machinery exclusively in the hands of the president or his Office of Management and Budget."[24] The Congressional Budget Office was considered for the job but rejected on constitutional grounds. Congressional negotiators gave responsibility for determining that the maximum allowable deficit under law would be exceeded, and thus the power to trigger the sequester process, to the General Accounting Office (GAO), the government's auditor. To ensure independence in auditing government accounts the GAO was positioned anomalously between the executive and legislative branches.

24. Havens, "Gramm-Rudman-Hollings," p. 10.

The head of the GAO, the comptroller general, is appointed by the president but is in large measure responsible to the Congress, which has the power to fire him. The organizational independence of the GAO and its reputation for impartiality made it an ideal agency to be trusted with the trigger.

There was a serious question whether this arrangement was legal, however. Immediately after Gramm-Rudman was signed into law, Representative Mike Synar (D-Okla.) brought suit in federal court, challenging the law on constitutional grounds.[25] The district court panel of three judges that considered the case in early 1986 ruled that, by vesting the power to trigger the sequester process in the comptroller general, the act violated the constitution. The president appoints the comptroller general, but the capacity of Congress to remove the head of the GAO made that office subservient to Congress.[26]

The Supreme Court, acting with dispatch, promptly heard arguments in the case (*Charles A. Bowsher v. Mike Synar et al.*) and affirmed the district court ruling by a 7–2 decision. The court declared the automatic reduction procedure "unconstitutional on the ground that it vests executive power in the Comptroller General, an officer removable by Congress." In this case the court argued—as it did in *Chadha v. INS* (1983)—that the legislative branch may legally issue binding directions to the

25. Anticipating the constitutional challenge, the drafters of Gramm-Rudman had written into the law rules providing for expedited judicial review. See *The Congressional Budget Process: A General Explanation* (1986), pp. 105–106.

26. See Lance T. LeLoup, Barbara Luck Graham, and Stacey Barwick, "Deficit Politics and Constitutional Government: The Impact of Gramm-Rudman-Hollings," *Public Budgeting and Finance* (Spring 1987):83–103, for a lucid account of the progress of Gramm-Rudman through the courts.

executive branch only through enacting a law that may be vetoed by the president: "To permit the execution of laws to be vested in an officer answerable only to Congress would, in practical terms, reserve in Congress control over the execution of laws. . . . The structure of the constitution does not permit Congress to execute the laws; it follows that Congress cannot grant to an officer under its control what it does not possess."[27]

The court's decision killed Gramm-Rudman. Without the comptroller general's report to the president, the automatic quality of the plan was lost, and unless the deficit ceilings were automatically enforced they would not be enforced at all.[28]

Anticipating that the comptroller general's report would not be constitutional, Gramm-Rudman incorporated a backup provision that called upon both House and Senate Budget Committees, acting as a Joint Committee, to initiate legislation directing the president to effect the sequestration. This would be constitutional because the president would have the opportunity to veto the triggering legislation and stop the process. But the backup plan was flawed: it allowed Congress to decide whether to enforce the deficit ceiling.[29]

27. Quoted in ibid., p. 97.
28. When the Supreme Court struck down Gramm-Rudman in 1986, it also ruled the March sequesters unconstitutional. Congress had to act to preserve that sequester, which it did by passing a bill to take the place of the comptroller general's report. See *CQ Almanac, 1986*, p. 580.
29. The maximum allowable deficit for FY 1987 was $144 billion. In August 1987 a CBO-OMB report indicated that the deficit would be approximately $163.4 billion, nearly $20 billion over the target, and called for across-the-board sequesters of 5.6 percent in defense programs and 7.6 percent in unprotected domestic programs. However, because the law allows for a margin of error of $10 billion Congress only had to reduce the projected deficit by $10 billion. The Joint Committee prepared resolutions to initiate the sequester, but

Gramm-Rudman was dead, but it would not stay in the grave. The Reagan administration had been pleased at the Supreme Court decision striking down the enforcement provision. Although the president had warmly embraced the concept of an automatic budget balancing plan, shortly after he signed the bill into law the Justice Department joined the side of Mike Synar and others to have the bill overturned. But in summer 1987 the government again ran out of borrowing authority, creating the need for another bill to increase the debt ceiling. Phil Gramm announced his intention to use this as an opportunity to fix the trigger and revive his budget-balancing plan. Of his determination to revive his plan for automatic budgetary balance, Gramm said, "this is a war that is not going to be called off."[30] The administration, displeased that the defense buildup might again be threatened by automatic cuts, privately lobbied Gramm to end his crusade against deficits. Insinuating that his efforts would comfort the Russians, administration representatives reportedly asked Gramm to abandon his effort in order "to keep Ivan from the gate." Gramm noted that "there are certainly people at the Pentagon who are nervous about it."[31] But he did not relent.

Political forces aligned rather differently the second time around for Gramm-Rudman. In 1985 the Republicans in Congress had been in the vanguard while Dem-

---

Congress did not enact them, claiming that a pending reconciliation bill would satisfy the deficit target. The projected deficit in FY 1987 was so close to the Gramm-Rudman target because of a one-time revenue windfall from enacting the 1986 tax bill. See *CQ Almanac, 1986*, p. 580.

30. *CQ Weekly Report*, July 18, 1987, p. 1571.
31. *CQ Weekly Report*, Aug. 8, 1987, p. 1789.

ocrats tagged along in the background. In 1987 roles were partially reversed. Prominent Democrats were among the plan's most energetic supporters while Republican leaders hung back and voiced their growing doubts. Senate Budget Committee chairman Lawton Chiles (D-Fla.) and Ways and Means Committee chairman Dan Rostenkowski both supported the revival of Gramm-Rudman because they believed that the threat of defense cuts would force the president to accept tax increases. As Rostenkowski explained, "When you want to get somebody's attention, kick his dog."[32] In his capacity as Ways and Means Committee chairman, Rostenkowski had special problems that he believed Gramm-Rudman might help solve. The FY 1988 budget resolution called upon the tax committees to produce legislation yielding $19.3 billion in new revenues in the first year and $63 billion over three years. Reagan, true to form, swore again and again that he would veto any tax increase. Members of the Ways and Means Committee were naturally reluctant to vote for any tax increase, but the likelihood that their labors would only provide the president with an opportunity to veto a Democratic tax increase and denounce Congress anew made them quite unwilling to vote for new taxes. Gramm-Rudman was useful to Rostenkowski because it might make the president more likely to sign a tax bill, and that in turn would make it easier to get a tax bill out of the Ways and Means Committee.

Bennett Johnston continued to argue that the president would not cave in to threats. He was joined in his opposition by a substantial number of Democratic senators as well as by a surprising new ally, former Senate

32. *CQ Weekly Report,* July 11, 1987, p. 1515.

Budget Committee chairman Pete Domenici (R-N.M.), who had ardently supported Gramm-Rudman in 1985. He had come to the view that President Reagan was so strongly opposed to tax increases that he would rather risk the sequester process than accept taxes. Skepticism about the wisdom of Gramm-Rudman was reportedly widespread among Republicans, but because they were so closely identified with the proposal and had argued for it so strongly in 1985, it would be extremely embarrassing for Republicans to defect wholesale in 1987. The president was similarly trapped by his previous words and deeds. Having frequently berated Congress for its supposed irresponsible ways and having repeatedly asked Congress for a balanced budget constitutional amendment, he could not veto a balanced budget proposal without losing face.[33]

Despite such deep misgivings the proposal moved forward through the legislative process. On September 23 the House passed, 230–176, a new, improved, and constitutionally sound Gramm-Rudman budget-balancing law; the Senate did likewise, 64–34. The president signed it into law, and Washington stepped into the ring for another round with Grammbo. The Gramm-Rudman "fix" set FY 1993 as the new year of the balanced budget, as opposed to FY 1991 in the original.[34] It avoided the constiutional difficulties of its predecessor by vesting the power to trigger sequesters in the Office of Management and Budget, an agency unambiguously executive in nature.

33. *CQ Weekly Report,* Sept. 19, 1987, p. 2234.
34. The revised schedule of maximum deficits was: FY 1988—$144 billion; FY 1989—$136 billion; FY 1990—$100 billion; FY 1991—$64 billion; FY 1992—$28 billion; FY 1993—no deficit!

Does the Sequester Threat Encourage Compromise?

In 1987 as they had in 1985, the supporters of Gramm-Rudman claimed it would force Congress and the president to compromise with each other, if only to prevent disaster. This logic, however, was never fairly tested, and it is unlikely that it ever would be. If a member of Congress values the protection and preservation of an individual program more than balancing the budget, he or she would never vote to subject the program to automatic reductions. Someone who values deficit reduction above particular components in the budget would not need Gramm-Rudman. Accordingly, as Gramm-Rudman made its way through Congress its evolution was similar to that of budget resolutions. To ensure majority acceptance in two chambers, more and more programs were protected from cuts. By the time the proposal had been amended in the Senate and gone through a conference committee it was greatly altered. To gain the support of liberals, programs providing benefits to the poor were exempted from cuts. To gain the support of southern Democrats, veterans' programs were protected. Reagan, of course, retained the power to prevent tax increases.

Gramm-Rudman was intended to end a logjam, to break an impasse, and to encourage compromise. But by the time the negotiations were ended and the bill passed, the programs that members cared about most were protected from sequestration. There was no increased incentive to negotiate. Individuals who wanted most of all to protect Social Security could do so, as before, by refusing to negotiate. The evolution of Gramm-Rudman from a proposal under which all programs would suffer to one under which some programs were protected concerned Representative Trent Lott: "Once we exempted certain programs from sequestration . . . we made the automatic spending cut approach more thinkable and doable, and we made it that much less likely that Congress would face up to its responsibilities to order priorities and make those cuts in a more reasoned and reasonable manner."[35] Under sequesters, President Reagan's defense budget would take a beating, but he could still ensure through his veto that taxes would not rise. Gramm-Rudman would not initiate, as Representative Boulter hoped, "the beginning of a great national debate to force us to make choices."[36] Instead, Congress made its choices and set its priorities in deciding what programs to exempt from the sequester process.

Fall 1987 provided the first good test of the notion that Gramm-Rudman would encourage compromise, and the test confirmed the fears of Bennett Johnston and Pete Domenici. The new rules for sequesters required minimum deficit reductions of $23 billion in FY 1988 to prevent sequestration. The Democrats pushed a reconciliation bill (including $12.3 billion in new revenues) through Congress. While this bill, if enacted, would partly satisfy Gramm-Rudman, it did not satisfy the president, who promised to veto it. Republicans in Congress wondered openly why the Democrats even bothered to complete action on the measure.

Once again the political system was deadlocked. The Democratic offer, the reconciliation bill, was on the table, but it was rejected outright by the president. Reagan and other Republicans let it be known that they pre-

35. *Cong. Rec.*, daily edition (Dec. 11, 1985), p. H11878.
36. Ibid., p. H11884.

ferred to allow the across-the-board reductions to take place than to consider higher taxes. "Arithmetic suggests that defense may not do much worse under automatic cuts than under conventional legislation in the Democratic led Congress," *Congressional Quarterly* reported. There were also signficant advantages to allowing the sequesters to proceed: "Under automatic cuts, they get the reductions in domestic programs that Reagan sought, no tax increase and many opportunities to blame Democrats for savaging the military."[37] Democrats saw political advantages for themselves in the situation, expecting that if Reagan vetoed their reconciliation bill and allowed the sequestration to occur, the public would blame Republicans. In addition, they liked the idea of cutting defense.

The bargaining and compromise that the proponents of Gramm-Rudman had so confidently predicted was nowhere to be seen. Both sides seemed more concerned with protecting their constituencies and their reputations than with actually balancing the budget or reducing the deficit. Both sides gave every appearance of happily accepting the "train wreck" in order to blame it on the opposition. This was politics as usual.

Sequestration would surely have taken place in 1987 but for the intervention of a random event—a stock market crash of over 500 points in just one day. On "Black Monday," October 19, a long bull market came to a sudden and sickening end as Wall Street experienced its biggest single day decline in stock prices.[38] Stock

37. *CQ Weekly Report*, Oct. 3, 1987, p. 2394.
38. In the Black Monday crash, the Dow Jones Industrial average lost 22.6 percent of its value, nearly twice the 12.8 percent decline in stock value of "Black Tuesday," October 28, 1929. Approximately $500 billion of wealth was lost in the decline. *CQ Weekly Report*, Oct. 24, 1987, p. 2573.

markets around the globe tumbled similarly, and the world wondered whether this was an accident or the precursor of bigger declines yet to come. In the days following the crash the market exhibited tremendous volatility, generating concern about what could be done to restore investor confidence and avert an all-out disaster. As stockbrokers, economists, politicians, and newspaper columnists sought to explain the event, they gladly heaped blame on the large federal deficit and the inability of Washington to control it.

The onset of Gramm-Rudman automatic spending reductions on October 20 underscored the impression that Washington was incapable of dealing responsibly with pressing political problems. According to Warren Rudman, "the falling of the Gramm-Rudman . . . ax tells [Wall Street] that the government isn't working, and that they don't want to hear." [39] The sequester order was issued by the president on October 15 but would not become permanent until November 20. Congress and the president had until then to produce deficit reductions worth $23 billion in order to roll back the sequester. Whether or not they could avert sequestration quickly became invested with tremendous significance.

To say that the stock market turmoil resulted from the federal budget deficit was ludicrous because the market had been on a steady rise for several years, in each of which there had been a very large deficit. Nonetheless, the budget deficit immediately became a popular scapegoat for the disaster, with members of Congress agreeing that the failure of the government to reduce deficits was at least partly responsible. President Reagan held a press conference within days of Black Monday and an-

39. Ibid., p. 2571.

nounced that he would meet with congressional leaders in an effort to reduce the deficit, "with everything on the table."[40] Bipartisan meetings began on October 26. The stock market had done what Gramm-Rudman could not—it introduced a sense of panic and desperation that made deficit reduction a high priority.

With the financial markets in a continuing turmoil, and with Wall Street watching and waiting, the budget negotiators began their meetings under tremendous pressure to agree. "A sense of apprehension, even fear, seems to have gripped negotiators on all sides of the table," Steven Roberts of the *New York Times* reported. "With the financial markets watching their every move, lawmakers say this is not the time to play their usual political games with the budget."[41] Bennett Johnston explained that among the negotiators "the feeling is that the markets are really looking at what we're doing. We're very conscious of the markets." An unnamed Republican senator expressed hope that Wall Street remained depressed because "that's the only way we'll get together. We've got to keep the pressure on."[42] The pressure was kept on by the opinion of a partner at the investment firm of Goldman, Sachs & Company, widely shared, according to the *New York Times*, that "the market would react negatively to a budget cut of only $20 billion." A Wall Street economist said that a cut of only $23 billion, the minimum needed to avert sequestration, "certainly cannot help the markets."[43]

40. R. W. Apple, Jr., "Reagan Says He'll Negotiate With Congress on the Deficit," *New York Times*, Oct. 23, 1987, p. 1.

41. Steven Roberts, "Parley on Budget Opened," *New York Times*, Oct. 29, 1987, p. 29.

42. Ibid.

43. Robert A. Bennett, "Wall St. Sees Market Drop in a Small Budget Cut," *New York Times*, Nov. 19, 1987, p. 15.

The goal of the conferees was to produce a reduction in the deficit of greater magnitude than the $23 billion sequester, and to this end they continued meeting over a period of several weeks. The negotiations were not easy, for Democrats continued to protect their favorite programs while the Republicans tried to protect their. But the talks held out promise of producing an agreement because, for now at least, all sides were less interested in scoring political points and more interested in reaching an agreement. The White House showed new flexibility on tax increases and Democrats showed greater flexibility on domestic spending. By November 10 one participant could say that "I think people see the outlines of a plan through the mist,"[44] and on November 20 an agreement on a deficit reduction of $30 billion was signed. The agreement called for $11 billion in revenue increases and spending cuts of $12.8 billion, of which $5 billion would come from defense. A variety of other measures, including $5 billion in asset sales, brought the total up to $30 billion. This was larger than the absolute minimum necessary to halt sequestration but not as large as some negotiators had hoped for. Apparently the group had come close to agreement on a much larger reduction involving highly controversial limits on entitlement COLAs, "but the idea was dropped when neither administration negotiators nor congressional leaders could figure out how to limit the political damage to their colleagues' satisfaction."[45]

Briefly, the stock market crash increased the importance to legislators of reducing the deficit and increased

44. Jonathan Feuerbringer, "Accord Held Near on Deficit Figures," *New York Times*, Nov. 11, 1987, p. 1.
45. Jonathan Feuerbringer, "Agreement Signed to Reduce Deficit $30 Billion in 1988," *New York Times*, Nov. 21, 1987, p. 1.

their willingness to exchange program reductions for deficit reductions. For once, it appeared that the cost of not reducing the deficit might be real and terrible. Constituents did not create much incentive to reduce the deficit, but the possibility of another stock market crash did. However, as the impact and memory of the horrors of Black Monday began to recede, the willingness to compromise declined accordingly.

The passage of Gramm-Rudman can be taken as evidence of the futility of the budget process and reconciliation. Because the budget process did not work, it can be argued, Gramm-Rudman was needed. However, Gramm-Rudman in 1987 shows how effective the reconciliation process is. When there was a general agreement, not just on the desirability of reducing the deficit, but on the means as well, the reconciliation mechanism facilitated its speedy enactment. After the 1987 summit agreement emerged, the House and Senate moved to implement its provisions by passing a reconciliation bill and a continuing appropriation.

The reconciliation bill included a number of controversial spending reductions, yet its enactment was never in serious danger. Members of the Senate Agriculture Committee were required by the agreement to produce $2.1 billion in savings over two years. They did not want to, but they did. "It is a chaotic situation," Senator David Pryor (D-Ark.) said. "We're about to make some very bad decisions for farmers and rural America because there is a gun at our head. The leadership has drawn a box around us, with tight parameters."[46] Enacting the package of deficit reductions might have been endangered had Republicans revolted and refused

46. Ward Sinclair, "Senate Panel Agrees to Cut Farm Programs," *Washington Post*, Dec. 5, 1987 (LEGI-SLATE Story No. 53059).

to support them because of included tax increases. Speaker Jim Wright announced that votes would be "needed on both sides of the aisle." Whether the legislation would pass depended, in Wright's view, on the level of support it received from the president.[47] House Minority Leader Bob Michel and President Reagan were able to persuade sufficient numbers of their own party to support the package; it passed both chambers and became law.

The summit agreement as implemented satisfied Gramm-Rudman in fact as well as on paper. The "maximum deficit amount" for FY 1988 was $144 billion, which, with a cushion of $10 billion added, meant that the deficit could be no larger than $154 billion. The actual deficit for the year was $155.1 billion. The $1.1 billion excess is exceedingly modest by congressional standards.

When deficit reduction does not appear to be the top priority of most members of Congress or the president, and when legislators seem more concerned with protecting programs that benefit their constituents, what can be expected of budgetary procedures? Very little, it would appear. As Tom Foley (D-Wash.) had said in the debate over Gramm-Rudman: "No rule or statute or constitutional amendment can require human beings to agree to something."[48]

47. Mary Thornton, "Wright Says Deficit Bill Needs GOP Votes," *Washington Post*, Nov. 23, 1987 (LEGI-SLATE Story No. 52342).
48. *CQ Weekly Report*, June 6, 1987, p. 1173.

Conclusion: Budgetary Procedure and Political Outcomes

Of the many theories to explain the outbreak of World War I, one of the more novel is Edward Fitzpatrick's contention that the war resulted from Germany's use of the executive budget. In 1918 he wrote: "Without the executive budget the dominant Prussian military caste could never have permeated the German people with its immoral ideas and made Germany synonymous with organized terror and frightfulness. . . . With a Reichstag with real control over the purse strings, Germany could never have attained her present position as an outlaw among nations."[1] Like Fitzpatrick, students and observers of Congress have commonly relied on procedure and organization as explanatory variables. Lacking a clear understanding of the role of procedure in politics, they have often committed the same sort of misattribution of results to procedural causes as Fitzpatrick. Procedures clearly have an impact on outcomes, but one must avoid attributing all institutional failures to procedural inadequacies.

Since 1974, members of Congress have been engaged in a continuing quest to improve their budgeting sys-

1. Edward Fitzpatrick, *Budget Making in a Democracy* (New York: Macmillan, 1918), p. ix.

tem, in hopes of producing better policy. These efforts have been guided by an implicit, largely unexamined theory of the relationship of procedure to politics—a theory that led them to attribute dysfunction in congressional budgeting to procedural and organizational inadequacies. This is not a unique interpretation. For decades, congressional observers have developed the theme that various aspects of the internal arrangements of Congress, especially the committee and seniority systems, preclude the emergence of majorities or keep existing majorities from getting their way. Instead of engaging in vigorous action in response to national problems, Congress has often been deadlocked, incapable of acting. With respect to the budget, critics and members of Congress have taken the position that the inability of Congress to act swiftly and decisively, or sometimes at all, is likewise due to procedural causes. Budgetary problems are thus often believed amenable to procedural solutions because the disagreeable outcomes are seen as a product of the procedures. The budget reforms adopted since 1974 have increased the power of congressional majorities: helping overcome a lack of coordination in budgeting that weakened Congress vis-à-vis the executive; providing Congress with procedures that permit adopting a far more coherent budget policy than previously possible; and enabling Congress to exercise more deliberate control over the budget and deficit. Now, what majorities want to accomplish in the budget, they can.

The structural and procedural changes brought about by the Budget Act of 1974 have been striking, but the budgetary consequences of these structural changes have been less impressive. The congressional budget process, even with its exceptionally majoritarian fea-

ional and consistent it is still possible
f a lack of agreement and an unwilling-
omise, individual budgetary preferences
y be aggregated into a single budget policy
a majority. It is entirely possible that, even
do have individually rational preferences,
e no one budget on which a majority can
ously, the less consensus there is and the less
re open to compromise, the more remote are
reaching agreement. If a substantial minor-
right insists, for instance, on increasing de-
nding and not raising taxes, and another mi-
the left refuses cutting social programs and all
balancing the budget, then there may be no
y in the middle. Majorities may even support
omponent of the budget—on taxes, defense, So-
curity, and so forth—but these issue-oriented ma-
s need not aggregate into majority support of a
rehensive budget policy.

his exact problem plagued Congress through the
0s, making the passage of budget resolutions a pro-
cted legislative adventure. In both parties organized
oups on the left and the right did, and do, doom bud-
t resolutions, by refusing to vote with their colleagues.
epublican "Gypsy Moths," representing the Northeast
n the House, are relatively liberal and fight for the preservation of Amtrak subsidies and other regional issues.
"Yellow Jackets" are Republican conservatives in the
House, mostly from the South, who fight for the Reagan
agenda of low taxes and high defense. "Boll Weevils" are
conservative Southern Democrats who have sided with
Reagan and the Republican party in the House on many
key votes. With the majority party often having only a
slim command of the chamber, relatively few defections

tures, has not reduced dissastisfaction with congressional handling of the budget. Since 1974, budget deficits have been larger, not smaller; appropriations bills
have been enacted later, not earlier; overall spending
has gone up, not down; and the use of continuing resolutions and supplemental appropriations has increased,
not decreased. Despite universal displeasure with the
size of budget deficits for the past decade, Congress has
been mostly unable to undertake substantial deficit reduction measures. Judged by nearly any conceivable
output criteria, the budget process has not solved the
budget problem.

Yet we need not assume that congressional inability
to produce a satisfactory budget necessarily reflects procedural problems. Before condemning the budget process we should consider the possibility that the problem
inheres in the structure of preferences, not the procedures.[2] The congressional budget process is premised
not only on the view that decentralization of congressional spending power led to adverse consequences but
also on the assumption that congressional majorities
are capable of passing a responsible budget, if only
given the chance. Such majorities do not necessarily exist; if they do not, one should not expect satisfactory
budgets to emerge from Congress, regardless of the procedures employed. When the procedures favor majorities, passing a budget may prove difficult if stable majorities are not present.

2. This argument is related to, but different than, the problems of
collective choice discovered by Kenneth Arrow and others. The issue
here is not "cycling," but an inability to agree on both items and totals. But as William Riker points out, these scholars discovered that
"tastes" as well as procedures could be problematic. "Implications
from the Disequilibrium of Majority Rule for the Study of Institutions," *American Political Science Review* 74 (June 1980): 432–458.

There are two different sources for collective indecisiveness in Congress on the budget. First, possibly member preferences on the budget are irrational or inconsistent, and an individual member finds no budget satisfactory in both its total amount of spending and taxing and its distribution of spending. There is a well-known paradox of public opinion: within individuals, preferences on the total level of spending are often inconsistent with preferences on programs. Most survey respondents contend that the total level of public spending is "too high," even when they support raising or maintaining current levels of spending on most programs. The only components of public spending perceived as too high are welfare and foreign aid, two small but very unpopular categories of spending.[3] If member budgetary preferences are similarly inconsistent—with an insistence on small deficits, low taxes, and few or no budget cuts—budgetary deadlock would hardly be surprising. Political attitudes among elites are more consistent and stable than among nonelites, but they are not necessarily consistent.[4] Consider the following discussion of a well-known conservative member of the House, who has argued vigorously in favor of dismantling the welfare state and replacing it with a "conservative opportunity society."

> Newt Gingrich (R-Ga.) . . . says that opposing cuts in what to the naked eye look like Liberal Welfare State programs is the best way to promote the Con-

3. For evidence of the apparent irrationality of public attitudes toward public spending, see David Sears and Jack Citrin, *Tax Revolt: Something for Nothing in California* (Cambridge: Harvard University Press, 1982).

4. Herbert McClosky et al., "Issue Conflict and Consensus Among Party Leaders and Followers," *American Political Science Review* 54 (1960): 406–427.

servati
conserv
was also
in his dist
surely do.
grich a "dea
ber wanted h
House membe
pathetic," Ging
involved right nc
beating up on me.
paper stapled toge
tionnaire of what yo
she said. . . . Gingric
piciously. Like most cc
endorsing specific bud
quently supports a bala
to send this in?" he asked.

More than the mass publ
should understand that baland
quire painful choices. But give
budget-balancing measures, me
often prefer to maintain a clearly i
ically inconsistent position, opposin
welfare state but supporting the pr
prise it. The presence of such members
plicates the task of finding a majority to
get.[6]

Second, and more troubling, even if in

5. Nicholas Lemann, "Conservative Opportunity S
tic, May 1985, p. 25.

6. According to David Stockman, President Reagan
hibited inconsistent attitudes on the budget and defi
amusing discussion of how Reagan flunked an "exam" on t
The Triumph of Politics (New York: Harper & Row, 1986),
357.

can pose a major problem. The Republican party in the Senate was particularly subject to defection after 1981 given their extremely thin majority. On the right, a handful of stalwart Reagan supporters refused to budge on the issue of taxes, while a small group of relatively liberal Republicans was opposed to the size of the defense budget and sought to prevent big cuts in domestic spending. The problem for the Republican leadership was that it could not afford to lose the support of either group; if it did, then it no longer formed a majority. Democrats made matters worse by refusing to support Republican resolutions and cheerfully stood back to watch the Republicans squirm and struggle.

The comprehensive nature of budget resolutions increases the difficulty of passing a budget. Unless issue majorities tend to coincide, the aggregative decision making of the budget resolutions may actually discourage the emergence of agreement.[7] To obtain agreement on a budget resolution, a comprehensive document, requires far greater party cohesion than passing a budget piece by piece. Under the budget process a single majority must simultaneously agree on the level of spending, the distribution of spending among programs, the level of revenue, and the size of the deficit. But parties and coalitions in Congress are normally far from cohesive. Instead of relying on the same coalition again and again on one bill after another, leaders face the responsibility of building a new coalition for every bill.[8] A group of leg-

7. Riker explains, "the popular will is defined only as long as the issue dimensions are restricted. Once issue dimensions multiply, the popular will is irresolute." William Riker, *Liberalism Against Populism* (San Francisco: W. H. Freeman, 1982), p. 241.

8. Barbara Sinclair, "Building Coalitions in the Sand," in *The New Congress*, ed. Thomas Mann and Norman Ornstein (Washington, D.C.: American Enterprise Institute, 1981), pp. 178–220.

islators who agree on one aspect of the budget will probably not agree on all aspects. A legislator who finds one
aspect of an omnibus appropriation or budget bill exceedingly obnoxious may feel compelled to vote against
the entire bill. But if the appropriations are split into
multiple bills he or she will be forced to vote against
only one. Multiply this one stubborn legislator many
times, and the prospects for passing an omnibus bill begin to decline. The genius of the old practice of considering the budget only in pieces, never as a whole, was
that it minimized the possibility of stalemate.

Structural Consequences of Weak Parties

Critics point to the slowness of Congress, its tendency to
stalemate, the absurdities of the filibuster, attributing
these and other problems to legislative procedure. Yet it
would be incorrect to assume that removing opportunities for obstruction would radically transform the behavior of Congress. The structural complexity of Congress and the opportunities for obstruction were neither
imposed by an external force nor retained through force
of habit. Congress determines its own rules, and it is
fully capable of eliminating procedures and arrangements that do not serve its members' purposes. If a majority wants to legislate more speedily, it can adopt appropriate rules.

To a limited degree fragmentation of congressional
organization thwarts majorities, but to a far greater extent the absence of stable majority coalitions has led to
adopting fragmented and decentralized legislative institutions. The filibuster in the Senate may appear a
medieval relic, but its persistence into the late twentieth
century and the strong support it receives from liberals

and conservatives, Democrats and Republicans alike, reflects the uncertainties of congressional coalitions. A senator who expects to be in the minority on some issue of great importance will support the filibuster as a means of protecting those vital interests. A large majority of senators can expect to be in the minority on some issue they deem crucial, whether it be tax policy, agriculture price supports, tobacco supports, merchant marine subsidies, tariffs, or any of dozens of policies. And so the filibuster endures.

Unable to rely on strong legislative parties capable of formulating and passing a coherent program, it has been incumbent upon members of Congress to adopt decentralized structures—a strong committee system—as a means of building ad hoc coalitions. James Sterling Young finds the origins of congressional decentralization in the absence of an organizing force following the end of the Jefferson administration. In describing a Congress that was chaotic, disorganized, unstable, and characterized by warring factions and weak parties, Young could as well be describing the Congress of today.

> The eclipse of the Presidency after Jefferson signified the loss of the only stabilizing influence then available upon a governing society on the Hill. . . . The party did not evolve toward an organized action group, toward greater cohesion, once Jefferson's leadership had collapsed. On the contrary, loss of presidential leadership was attended by disintegration of the majority party into warring factions, by an accelerating fragmentation of the social and political system on Capitol Hill, and by the development of a committee system which not merely introduced new divisive forces but also offered legislators a means of exercising power which

minimized the need for building stable majority coalitions.[9]

In short, lacking parties or a strong executive, Congress
developed committees. Decentralized organization permitted the accomplishment of limited, meliorative purposes while avoiding complete stalemate. Adopted to
lessen the problems that accompany a lack of consensus,
decentralization in turn has been the cause of other
problems: slowness, unrepresentativeness, narrow perspective, and frequent stalemate.

Discussing the Italian Parliament, Giuseppe DiPalma
explains how the committees, although far less important than those in the U.S. Congress, nonetheless encourage compromise and agreement. Summarizing a poll he
took of Italian legislators, DiPalma writes: "They began
by praising the informality surrounding committee
work, which makes the public demagoguery characteristic of floor debates unnecessary or out of place. They
found that the relative privacy of the committees allowed their members to put aside, for once, general
principles and to search for agreement. They appre-
ciated the fact that committee work puts a premium on
solving issues and making decisions, as against elo-
quence, ideology, and partisan pressure."[10]

A committee system and the concomitant wide dis-
persal of legislative power tend to encourage agreement
on legislation of limited scope. However, decentralized
organization affords committees the ability to frustrate
such majorities as from time to time emerge. Formally,

9. James Sterling Young, *The Washington Community, 1800–1829*
(New York: Columbia University Press, 1966), pp. 209–210.
10. Giuseppe DiPalma, *Surviving Without Governing: The Italian
Parties in Parliament* (Berkeley: University of California Press, 1976),
p. 198.

at least, the discharge petition enables majorities in the House to overcome obstreperous committees.[11] But members have often preferred not to offend the committee in question, so the discharge petition has been little used. For instance, only after the House Judiciary Committee had refused for twenty-two years to schedule hearings on the Equal Rights Amendment was a discharge petition used to bring the measure to the floor.[12]

If stable coalitions were to appear, the problems stemming from the procedural complexity of Congress would disappear. When committed majorities do arise, they are able to overcome the tendency toward stalemate, by either changing procedures or simply overwhelming minorities by strength of numbers. Experience with civil rights legislation after World War II indicates that conceding power to committees can keep majorities from getting their way. But it also shows that if the majority is relatively committed to its goal, it can change the rules and ultimately prevail.

Passage of civil rights legislation in the 1960s was made possible only by changing the rules in both the House and the Senate in order to deprive southern conservatives of the practical veto they held in each chamber. In the years after the Second World War, majorities in both House and Senate came to favor stronger civil rights laws, but in spite of several attempts they were unable to pass meaningful, enforceable legislation to

11. Paul Hasbrouck describes the origins of the discharge petition; his enthusiasm for this legislative device has not been vindicated. *Party Government in the House of Representatives* (New York: Macmillan, 1927), chap. 8, pp. 134–165.

12. Gilbert Steiner, *Constitutional Inequality: The Political Fortunes of the Equal Rights Amendment* (Washington, D.C.: Brookings Institution, 1985), pp. 12–21.

improve the condition of blacks in the South. In the Senate, southerners could block the passage of legislation by means of the filibuster, and the proponents of civil rights, though more than half of the body, did not have the two-thirds needed to invoke cloture and cut off the debate. In the House, Southern Democrats and conservative Republicans used their control of the Rules Committee to keep liberal legislation, including civil rights, from ever getting to the floor for a vote.

Strong civil rights laws were passed, in 1964 and 1965, but only after rules changes permitted the majorities to prevail. In the Senate, the threshold for cloture was reduced from two-thirds to three-fifths, just enough to deprive the South of a veto. In the House, the Rules Committee was expanded from twelve to fifteen members by adding two Democrats and one Republican. This action gave the liberals on the committee a majority, enough to approve liberal legislation and allow it to move to the floor, where it was passed.[13] Rules and structure are intervening variables, mediating between the preferences of members and what actually happens. Procedures cannot force things to happen, but they can certainly enable minorities to stop action, yet for only so long.

If the majority is very large and cohesive, its members will be able to pass their program regardless of the official rules. In 1933, when the Democrats in the Senate numbered 60 and the Republicans 35 (in the House there were 310 Democrats to 117 Republicans), committee obstruction of majority preference and the Roosevelt program was not a problem. Because of Democratic en-

13. This exciting contest for supremacy in the House is documented in Neil MacNeil, *The Forge of Democracy* (New York: McKay, 1963), pp. 410–448, and Richard Bolling, *House Out of Order* (New York: Dutton, 1965), pp. 195–220.

thusiasm for the new administration, no committee was far out of tune with the chamber's melody.[14] Procedural obstructionism will typically only be a problem when the majority is small. Upon occasion a large majority comes into Congress and acts aggressively and quickly, as if the decentralized procedures were not there. The Democrats in 1933 were able to do this, as they were again in 1965; in both cases, the Democratic majority was large and cohesive. But even huge numerical advantages for the Democrats in these cases did not ensure lasting dominance. In 1937, the Democratic margin was larger than ever, but by then party solidarity had diminished, and Roosevelt's legislative program encountered difficulties in Congress. In 1981, very small (but extremely cohesive) majorities were able to overcome the obstruction of committees, but only because the budget process had enormously centralized budget procedure and eliminated the possibility of committee obstruction. Unless they are very large and committed, whether majorities get their way is largely a matter of chance in a decentralized legislature.

When parties are strong and coalitions are stable the majority has neither need nor patience for the procedural complexity of a committee system. T. Harry Williams's account of the Louisiana state legislature at the height of Huey Long's power illustrates the role of committees where party is supreme:

Immediately after the bills were introduced in the house, all forty-four of them were referred to the

14. Robert Giaimo, former chairman of the House Budget Committee, claimed in testimony to the HBC that, in the first hundred days of the Roosevelt administration, Congress passed bills that had not yet been written. *Budget Process Review,* Hearings before the House Budget Committee, 97th Cong., 2nd sess. (USGPO, 1982), p. 94.

committee on ways and means. The committee met the next morning and reported them favorably in a session lasting only one hour and forty-two minutes, giving to each bill a consideration averaging only slightly more than two minutes. The bills were then rushed to the house floor, where they were enacted almost without debate and sent to the senate. In the upper chamber they were referred to the finance committee, which seemed determined to beat the house committee's record for speed. It passed favorably on the bills in one hour and twenty-one minutes. . . . The committee hearings were brief partly because only one witness appeared before both bodies—that interested citizen, Senator Long.[15]

Neither Huey nor any other party boss would put up with independent committees because they have no need to build consensus. When the parties or coalitions are sufficiently strong that members of the majority feel no particular need of minority protections, they streamline the legislative process to enable themselves to achieve their purposes. When the Republicans regained control of the House in 1889 and elected Thomas B. Reed of Maine as their Speaker, they were united on a legislative program and determined not to let the minority Democrats frustrate them. To prevent minority obstruction, Reed and the Republicans dramatically transformed the rules of the House, augmenting the power of the Speaker and reducing the minority's capacity to block legislation.[16] Twenty years later the Republican party split, and insurgent Progressive Republicans

15. T. Harry Williams, *Huey Long* (New York: Random House, 1969), pp. 739–740. The "antis" were the otherwise nameless faction opposed to the Long organization.

16. See William A. Robinson, *Thomas B. Reed: Parliamentarian* (New York: Dodd, Mead, 1930). Reed explained the problem of ob-

joined with the Democrats in the revolt against Speaker Joseph Cannon to reduce the power of the Speaker and the majority.[17]

Typically, procedural remedies are prescribed for whatever ails Congress, mindless of the extent to which the congressional procedures reflect the nature of coalitions in Congress. To know whether procedural reform will work, one must first know whether the problem is procedural in origin or the manifestation of fundamental characteristics of the political system. Did Germany's use of the executive budget cause the First World War? Or was the executive budget adopted because of underlying autocratic tendencies in German politics? If the latter is true, as most would suspect, then changing the budget would have done little to avert the war.

Without the presence of stable majorities, removing barriers to majority action will not directly result in better policy or more energetic legislative action. Time and again, writers on Congress have initially noted the profound sources of congressional fragmentation and

---

struction in the House: "A series of circumstances prior to 1890 had concurred to render the House of Representatives the most unwieldy parliamentary body in the world. The last revision [in the 46th Congress] had been made by distinguished men of both parties, but all animated ... by a desire that the minority should have great power. ... The motions to adjourn, to fix the day of adjournment, and to take a recess, being 'in order at all times,' constituted a barrier by which three resolute men could stop all public business. ... One member could move to take a recess, another to fix the time to adjourn, and the third to adjourn, and demand yeas and nays on each; each taking up three-quarters of an hour. [A]t the end the motions could be renewed and another three hours be destroyed, and so on until the majority, tired out, would surrender." Thomas B. Reed, *Reed's Rules: A Manual of General Parliamentary Law* (Chicago: Rand, McNally, 1898), pp. 213–214.

17. See Charles Atkinson, *The Committee on Rules and the Overthrow of Speaker Cannon* (New York: Columbia University Press, 1911); and Hasbrouck, *Party Government in the House of Representatives.*

then, in spite of their own analysis, have argued that congressional procedures keep it from acting. For example, in 1954 Professor Arthur Holcombe of Harvard, representing the American Political Science Association committee on party reform, testified before Congress that the procedures of Congress were not conducive to party government. Holcombe explained that failure to reform would result in diminution of congressional power with respect to the executive. His favored solution was to replace seniority as a means of selecting committee chairs with election in the party caucus. This, he said, would result in a "disciplined and efficient team of party leaders." At this point John McClellan of Arkansas, the committee chairman, interrupted:

THE CHAIRMAN: What do you mean by "disciplining Members of Congress"?

DR. HOLCOMBE: Simply the practice of acting together as a group of leaders—

THE CHAIRMAN: Acting together is one thing, but disciplining is another. What do you mean by "disciplining," Doctor?

DR. HOLCOMBE: Only in the sense of responsibility to the majority of the party.

THE CHAIRMAN: I just wondered about that, Doctor. I happen to be pretty independent and I know a lot of other members of Congress who happen to be pretty independent. No party or no leader is going to put a ring in my nose and tell me to vote this way or that way, as long as I am here.[18]

18. *Organization and Operation of Congress*, Hearings before the Senate Committee on Expenditures in the Executive Department, 82nd Cong., 1st sess. (USGPO, 1951), pp. 209–210.

Given the presence of "435 parties in the House," according to Thomas Foley,[19] how much can we expect from procedural reform? Certainly neither such changes as Holcombe recommends, nor any others one can imagine, will induce a renaissance of parties. Occasionally there is a voice of sanity. According to Gary Orfield, "liberals are unlikely to accomplish much by reforming congressional procedures. The sobering reality is that the real obstacles are not so much on Capitol Hill as in the society as a whole. . . . Most of the time, we have the Congress we really want and the Congress we deserve."[20] The capacity of procedural changes to alter legislative results is limited by the structure of coalitions in Congress, which are, in turn, largely determined by factors outside Congress.

There is no question but that congressional budgets produced by means of its extremely fragmented procedure prior to 1974 were unsatisfactory to large numbers of legislators. Each appropriations bill received at least majority support, and in most cases far more than the bare minimum needed to pass. Tax bills likewise passed easily, and so did legislation increasing entitlements. Each component of the budget was popular; but when members viewed the overall policy that resulted from the independent, uncoordinated actions, they were greatly displeased, both by the size of the budget and the magnitude of the deficit. Furthermore, members of Congress found themselves unable to agree to measures that would either increase taxes or reduce spending sufficiently to render the overall budget policy acceptable.

19. Quoted in Austin Ranney, ed., *The Referendum Device* (Washington, D.C.: American Enterprise Institute, 1981), p. 70.

20. Gary Orfield, *Congressional Power: Congress and Social Change* (New York: Harcourt, Brace, Jovanovich, 1975), pp. 9–10.

In these bad years for Congress, the budget truly was out of control.

From their words and actions, members of Congress apparently assumed in 1974 that there was a majority to support a sensible budget policy, which was, however, prevented from either emerging or getting its way by the fragmented budget procedures. To the extent that members expected the Budget Act to happily resolve the budget problem, they have been disappointed. Since the institution of reconciliation in 1980 there have been virtually unparalleled opportunities for majorities in Congress to remake public policy according to their desires. But after fifteen years with the new budget process, dissatisfaction with budget policy remained undiminished. The problem has not been a failure of the budget process to bring about sufficient centralization—for there is now an extraordinary degree of centralization—but a lack of majorities to take advantage of the procedures.

In 1981 Reagan's unexpected landslide electoral victory, his skillful politicking, and an assassination attempt, which caused his popularity to soar, combined to create a temporary majority in favor of large budget cuts. Congress acted with unsurpassed speed and vigor to pass the largest budget cut ever. American government looked more like a parliamentary system than it had at any time since the madcap times of Roosevelt's Hundred Days.

Subsequent to Reagan's extraordinary first year, those majorities disappeared. The budget process that worked so well and efficiently in 1981 became slow and cumbersome without vigorous majorities to make it go. Since then, rather than transform Congress into a well-oiled legislative machine, the budget process has resulted in delay, frustration, and embarrassment for Congress. In 1982 Reagan did not get his way with Congress on the budget, and this prompted him to complain about Congress's "Mickey Mouse budget process." Yet the process he complained of was the same one that made possible his magnificent victories the previous year. The process had not changed, only the willingness of members to go along with his budget recommendations.

A centralized budget process involves certain difficulties, notably the frustration that accompanies an absence of majorities. But when majorities appear, the results can be impressive. The new budget process has made Congress capable of legislative action virtually inconceivable under normal legislative procedure. Achieving the immense budget cuts contained in the reconciliation bill in 1981 would have been impossible without the consolidated procedures of the budget process. Nothing so dramatic has occurred in subsequent years, but in every year after 1980 the budget process has permitted enacting budget cuts (admittedly small ones compared to the size of the deficit). The problems that remain stem not from the procedures, but from both the weak unstable coalitions and the disorders induced by a system of checks and balances.

The problem of absent majorities is exceedingly intractable. Gramm-Rudman is an effort to resolve it by forcing disparate factions to agree. Thus far, however, Gramm-Rudman has not been successful. Sequesters took place in 1986 and would have taken place again in 1987 but for the intervention of a stock market crash, which induced a momentary spirit of cooperation in

Washington. But it is unlikely that a similar spirit of compromise will return without another looming disaster.[21]

Further procedural reforms are unlikely to achieve much. The two versions of Gramm-Rudman have already done much to tighten the enforcement of budget resolutions. Enforcement procedures could no doubt be improved still further. Improved enforcement, however, would not address the problem of inducing Congress and the president to use the process more actively. Clearly the budget resolutions are not perfectly enforced; all the savings recommended in the budget resolution are not achieved.

Other reformers suggest simplifying the process in various ways: eliminating redundant decisions; shifting all or part of the budget to a two-year cycle; combining the budget resolution, all appropriations, reconciliation, and tax legislation into a single omnibus budget bill. These reforms would address certain persistent complaints with the budget process—it takes too much time, it prevents committees from engaging in oversight, the same issues are debated and decided repeatedly. Representative David Obey has argued for replacing the budget process with a single budget bill that would roll all appropriations, tax, and reconciliation into a single massive bill. The advantage in this approach is the elimination of duplicative actions, but it would not make it any easier to agree on a budget. When

21. The National Economic Commission, a bipartisan group established in 1988 to produce agreement on deficit reductions, was completely unable to reach consensus. Absent an immediate threat, neither liberals nor conservatives were willing to forsake their favored programs in order to achieve deficit reduction. See Benjamin Friedman, "A Deficit of Civic Courage," *New York Review of Books*, June 1, 1989, pp. 23–26.

it was reenacted in 1987 Gramm-Rudman encouraged committees to experiment with two-year budgeting. This popular idea will likely be adopted. It will reduce the legislative burden each year and perhaps help to avoid legislative logjams, but it will not diminish the fundamental policy disagreements that prevent deficit reduction.

Scholars at the Brookings Institution have made many recommendations for improving the budget process. They were particularly concerned with the extraordinary complexity of the process, and they suggest simplifying the process by shifting to multiyear budgeting, by consolidating the authorizations and appropriations processes, and by encouraging Congress to avoid the minutia of budgeting and stick to broad policy decisions. They believe these reforms would make the process more efficient and more understandable. However, they carefully avoid claiming too much for procedural reform. "Reforms to the process," they argue, "cannot substitute for political will or for the exercise of leadership in working out compromises among warring parties. As long as the government sticks with a system under which power is divided between the president and Congress . . . the priorities of the president and Congress will occasionally conflict. Changes in the budget process are unlikely to cure this situation."[22]

The measures that would most ensure more effective use of the budget process and more progress toward a resolution of the budgetary crisis are not at all budgetary in nature. If in some future election one party gains control of the presidency and both houses of Congress, agreement on a significant budget producing major def-

22. Henry Aaron et al., *Economic Choices 1987* (Washington, D.C.: Brookings Institution, 1986), p. 126.

icit reduction will be far easier to achieve than it was in the Reagan years. If the political parties could be made more cohesive, or if presidents somehow were given greater influence over the members of their party in Congress, that too would make agreement more forthcoming. Reconciliation in the budget process creates a legislative environment conducive to party government; anything that would encourage forming strong parties would make the budget process work better. However, tinkering with the process itself is unlikely to be tremendously helpful.

The budget process has not eliminated dissatisfaction with the budget, but it has eliminated procedural obstructions to adopting a coherent budget. Given what we can expect from procedural change, the Budget Act has been a splendid success. All that is needed now is a Congress capable of using its budget process.

Index

enforcement of budget resolution, 92; and entitlements, 86, 96n; evasions of, 112, 165–166; few floor amendments, 159; focuses attention on aggregates, 164; and Gramm-Rudman, 216, 221; House reaction to, 107–108; instructions, 95–96, 96n; introduction of, 107–112, 135; as means of coordination, 101; and majority power, 94–95, 113–115, 240; makes cuts possible, 101, 241; moved to first resolution, 109; multiyear, 111n; and omnibus bills, 164; and party government, 244; as result of economic concerns, 108; said to force unwise choices, 221; and spending cuts, 113; and tax committees, 96; and tax increases, 113; timing of, 97, 108; use of in 1981, 118–119
Reconciliation legislation, 77; compared to budget resolution, 113–114; conference committee on, 97, 111; extraneous matter in, 112; impediments to enactment, 112; passage of, 97n, 111; timing of, 112
Reed, Thomas, B.: on obstruction in the House, 236–237n
Republicans: ambivalence about Gramm-Rudman, 214; attitudes toward spending cuts, 37n; budgetary concerns of, 80–81, 83–84; efforts to reduce spending in 1960s, 34–38; Gypsy Moths, 228; protest budget rules waivers, 75n; and spending ceiling, 39–50; Yellow Jackets, 228; voting

defections, 229; welcome sequestration, 216
Revenue sharing, 58–59
Revenues: actual compared with predicted, 91; Budget Committee consideration of, 68; and economic performance, 89
Riker, William, 54, 229
Roberts, Paul Craig, 80–82
Roosevelt, Franklin, 234
Rose Garden agreement, 116
Rostenkowski, Dan, 186, 213
Roth, William, 47
Rousselot, John, 71–72
Rudman, Warren, 186, 200, 217
Rules: governing appropriations, 26; waivers of, 75, 166

Safe districts: of Appropriations Committee members, 29–30
Sasser, James, 125
Schick, Allen, 32, 87, 102–103, 161, 193
Shultze, Charles, 52
Senate: ability to waive budget rules, 75; committees and reconciliation (1981), 120; disagrees with House and president, 40–41, 48, 112; passage of Budget Act, 78; sources of budget resolutions, 116–117
Senate Budget Committee (SBC): accommodation by, 104–105; and assumed legislative savings, 106–107; bipartisanship of, 103, 109; and budget process, 116; budget resolution in 1981, 118–119, 119n; deliberations of, 103–104; disagrees with president (1982), 123–124; floor success, 104; initiation of reconciliation by, 107; markup sessions,

Compositor: Graphic Composition, Inc.
Text: 11/14 Aster
Display: Helvetica Condensed & Aster
Printer: Maple-Vail Book Mfg. Group
Binder: Maple-Vail Book Mfg. Group